Cityscopes are concise, illustrated guides that provide an overview of a city's past as well as a focused eye on its present. Written by authors with unique and intimate knowledge of the cities, each book features a chronological history to the present day. Also including a section of essays on key places or aspects of the city today – from museums to music, public transport to parks, food to fashion – the books offer fascinating vignettes on the quintessential and the quirky, as well as listings of key sites and venues with the authors' own commentaries. Illustrated throughout with contemporary photos and compelling historical images, Cityscopes are essential companions to cities worldwide.

Titles in the series:

Beijing Linda Jaivin

Buenos Aires Jason Wilson

New York Elizabeth L. Bradley

cityscopes

NEW YORK

Elizabeth L. Bradley

REAKTION BOOKS

For Eric

Published by Reaktion Books Ltd
33 Great Sutton Street
London EC1V 0DX, UK

www.reaktionbooks.co.uk

First published 2015
Copyright © Elizabeth L. Bradley 2015

Printed and bound in China by Toppan Printing Co. Ltd

A catalogue record for this book is available from the British Library
ISBN 978 1 78023 342 0

OPENING IMAGES: pp. 6–7: looking over Central Park; p. 8: bronze statue of Atlas by Lee Lawrie, at the Rockefeller Center; p. 9: detail of the iconic crown design of the Chrysler Building; p. 10: the pedestrian plaza in Times Square; p. 11 (top): street signs on Broadway in SoHo; p. 11 (bottom): below-ground at Times Square is no less hectic than at street level; pp. 12–13: view of the Midtown skyline during Gay Pride in June, with the Empire State Building illuminated in rainbow colours; p. 14: aerial view of the High Line; p. 15: Bergdorf Goodman's holiday season window display; p. 16: classic brownstone facades in Harlem; p. 17: water-towers punctuate the New York skyline in almost every neighbourhood; p. 18 (top): walking the Mall in a wintry Central Park; p. 18 (bottom): the Coney Island boardwalk is less eccentric than it once was, but still attracts thousands each June for the Mermaid Parade; p. 19 (top): crosstown dog walkers; p. 19 (bottom): New York City Marathon runners crossing the Verrazano-Narrows Bridge.

CONTENTS

A view from Brooklyn: the Empire State Building seen through the Manhattan Bridge.

New Yorkers – native or adoptive – take it very much for granted that their city warrants all the superlatives and sobriquets that have been showered upon it throughout history. What other place, they insist, could simultaneously be Walt Whitman's 'Mighty Manhattan', Kander and Ebb's 'city that never sleeps', Jan Morris's 'world epitome', Le Corbusier's 'beautiful catastrophe' and Grandmaster Flash's 'big city of dreams'? New York's exceptionalism, and New Yorkers' (and others') endless drive to explain the city, have resulted in a nearly unrivalled cottage industry of museums, books, films, songs, TV shows, photo collections, exhibitions, websites, blogs, and even hashtags (#nyclife, #nycproblems). But is New York really so unique, now that Times Square belongs to Disney and there's an Apple Store in the Meatpacking District? Is the story of its colonization, capture and revolutionary overthrow so unusual? Why bother with another hymn to the city when the new, new thing is happening in Beijing or Mumbai? What sets New York apart in a global economy where, with the right technology, anyone can be a cosmopolite? It is not the only island city (Venice comes to mind), or even the only archipelago (Stockholm, Hong Kong). It no longer has the tallest skyscrapers (hello, Dubai) or the only 24/7 subway system (Chicago, Copenhagen). There is first-rate theatre to be seen elsewhere, and there are buzzy new restaurants around the globe. Why go to New York for the 'new Nordic cuisine' when you could go to Norway? Why go to MOMA when you can stream Marina Abramović's performance at home? The New York Stock Exchange still sits on Wall Street, to be sure, but automation has made it possible to trade on the 'Big Board' from anywhere. What monopoly does New York have? There are fashionistas in Paris, artists in London, visionaries in Tokyo, impresarios in Berlin and dealmakers and divas aplenty on the West Coast. Who cares what New York thinks of itself anymore?

The answer, for New Yorkers, is still 'everybody'. And why? Because the most polyglot city in the world is arguably the most protean: its physical and figurative landscapes are hard to catch and harder still to catalogue before they change again. So New York, in its delicious solipsism, can never stop articulating itself into existence, assessing its own historical impact and creating new reasons for non-residents to be surprised, intrigued or sometimes disgusted. How do New Yorkers *know* New York? Easy: like the famous definition of obscenity, they 'know it when they see it' – and hear it, and smell it, and taste it. New Yorkers find their authentic city in a growled pleasantry, an interrupted question or a piece of unsolicited advice; in the eternality of 'dirty water dogs', bodega cats and flying rats (also known as rock pigeons). They find it while stoop sitting, fire-escape leaning, subway sleeping – and in apartments so small they have to leave them to have a dinner party or a quarrel. The quest for the 'real' New York is the impetus behind innumerable bagel wars and pizza detentes. Favourite kosher deli? Keep it to yourself, for safety's sake. New York means proprietary feelings about parks, from the immense (Central, Prospect, Pelham Bay) to the infinitesimal (Septuagesimo Uno, 0.04 acres, 160 sq. metres, on the Upper West Side), and about bars (the artisanal, the Irish, the dive). It means hobbit-sized grocery stores with miniature shopping carts; hole-in-the-wall cobblers who moonlight making shoes for the Metropolitan Opera; and subway station agents who decorate their ticket booths for every holiday. It's fresh snow and fetid heat, all atop Manhattan schist. It's 'minding your own', except when minding everyone else's (and knowing how to time it right). It's stepping around the sidewalk prophets. It's the celebrity nod, which indicates to the famous person that the real New Yorker acknowledges them and will magnanimously leave them in peace at La

Bonbonniere with their coffee and the *Times*. It's kissing or crying or changing into heels in the back of a taxi speeding up the FDR Drive. It means leading a double life of day jobs and night passions (or just day and night jobs) and guessing that everyone else is, too. It's stirring a paper cup of 'regular' (milk and sugar) coffee by shaking it at arm's length. It's 'fuck' used as both sign and signifier. It's anything you desire at three in the morning, especially in the East Village. It's places to find quiet. Places to find noise. Places to be invisible. It's the plate tectonics of Manhattan real estate, rewarding and punishing the nostalgic in equal measure. It's knowing how to walk, and then walk some more: to 'be minimum', as Hart Crane wrote, the better to move quickly through a crowd, and to be a 'rover', per E. B. White, bearing witness to Gotham's everything. It's the joy of standing at the front of the head car of a subway train, barrelling through space, endlessly, beneath the frantic city.

At the beginning of Rem Koolhaas's *Delirious New York*, he makes what seems at first to be an outlandish assertion. 'I was Manhattan's ghostwriter,' he says, as if the city itself had put him on retainer to write an architectural manifesto. But there is, on reflection, nothing strange about Koolhaas's statement – it is the only natural response to New York's peculiar, anonymous allure. All New Yorkers, and all those who visit, write their version of the city's biography: it's the only way to bring the skyline down to size. And every resident, every visitor, is vehement in their assessment, whether flattering or not. The city invites dramatic reading. That is precisely what this book hopes to achieve, as well – to 'ghostwrite' New York, briefly and evocatively, for visitors and natives alike. Here the reader will find a concise and colourful history of the city's development from Dutch trading post to world capital, a capsule history that finds surprising points of connection across New York's 400-plus years, as well as meditations on themes germane to the contemporary city, including its natural landmarks, unnatural gin joints and immigrant enclaves. An annotated appendix offers suggestions for where to be and what to do, eat, hear and see in the

HISTORY

In the beginning, Manhattan was nothing special. The singular destiny of the island was not evident to Henry Hudson, as his triple-masted flyboat the *Halve Maen* (Half Moon) made its hopeful voyage into what is now New York Harbor, and up the North River. For the English explorer and his Dutch patrons, the river was all-important, not the forested and craggy land masses that they passed along the way. Stalwart as Odysseus with his ears stopped against the sirens' song, Hudson doggedly made his way upstream. He was not, however, looking for home, as Odysseus was, but for a short cut to China.

The fabled Northwest Passage to the Orient was the holy grail of explorers and investors alike in sixteenth- and seventeenth-century Europe, and many fruitless eastward trips in search of the Pacific Ocean ended up revealing bits and pieces of the Americas instead. Most, if not all, of these journeys were bankrolled by the governments and trading companies of England and the Netherlands, who sought to challenge the Spanish and Portuguese dominance of the Straits of Magellan. In fact, New York's first sighting by a European was the result of an earlier mistaken voyage: Giovanni da Verrazzano had first laid eyes on New York in 1524, when he was sailing for the French on the same mission as Hudson. Verrazzano had admired Manhattan's 'agreeable location' and dubbed it 'Angoulême' after the ancestral province of his patron, François I, but did not stay to explore the tidal estuary that bounded the island he saw – the same body of water that Hudson, more than 85 years later, was positive would take him to Cathay. The English explorer had promised as much to his employer, the Dutch East

India Company, which had funded his two previous and unsuccessful attempts to reach China via Greenland and Russia. But Hudson's third time was no charm: the mixed Dutch and English crew of the *Halve Maen* rowed up the river until they reached its headwaters, near Albany, only to find the narrowing channel too shallow for their ship to proceed. The 'inconstant soundings', as First Mate Robert Juet lamented in his journal, made further passage impossible, and Hudson and his crew headed back to the Atlantic Ocean, baffled in their cartography and disappointed in their quest.

What they had found was greater New York, a 'land pleasant with Grasse and Flowers, and goodly Trees, [and] very sweet smells', that was, from First Mate Juet's description, a kind of living cornucopia with plentiful grapes, pumpkins, corn, tobacco, beans, beavers and deer, while the waters were 'full of fish' and 'very good oysters'. The half-English, half-Dutch seamen of the *Halve Maen* did not, however, spend much time on this fragrant land. For the most part the sailors played it rather coy, staying on board ship and receiving the bounty of

A view of New Amsterdam as it appeared in 1673, from the cartographer Peter Schenk's *Hecatompolis* (1702).

this new country from the Lenape (Algonquin) people, who paddled dugout canoes to the ship to greet and trade with them. Hudson's relative lack of interest in exploring the banks of the river he had found may have been the by-product of his eagerness to reach the Northwest Passage, firm as he was in the belief that their final destination lay just a little further on. He may also have been discouraged by an attack, early in their sailing, on a party of his sailors exploring the coast: it resulted in the death of an English sailor named John Colman, and would become the first recorded murder in the history of colonial New York. In retaliation, the *Halve Maen* took two Lenape temporarily hostage, a tactical checkmate that set the stage for centuries of misunderstanding and enmity between Native Americans and these newest of New Yorkers.

Hudson, uninterested in North America, considered his trip a dramatic failure. The explorer's obsession with the Northwest Passage would ultimately be his undoing: he died just two years later in the icy waters of northeastern Canada, after being cast adrift in a small boat by his mutinous crew. The Dutch government, however, was more optimistic about the possibilities inherent in the estuary Hudson had discovered and the land masses that bounded it, and in 1614 the Dutch States General put out a call for 'diverse merchants, wishing to discover New Unknown Rivers, Countries and Places' to apply for the right to sail back to the region that the *Halve Maen* had accidentally found. The Dutch decision to return to the 'unknown' was driven almost entirely by the demand for a single commodity: beaver pelts. Seventeenth-century Europe depended on beaver fur to make hats and other articles of clothing, and the European beaver population had been decimated in the name of fashion. A new source for this coveted pelt made Hudson's thwarted voyage worth the trouble for the Dutch and for the handful of merchants who took up the States General's offer and bankrolled expeditions to the region, sight unseen. The squabbles of these early hunting parties over the allocation of pelts (which, more often than not, had been hunted not by the Dutch at all, but by the Lenapes, working on commission) ultimately led to the formation of the West

Henry Hudson statue in Henry Hudson Park, Spuyten Duyvil, the Bronx.

India Company (wic), which centralized the Dutch investment in privateering and colonization throughout the Americas and concentrated their resistance to the colonial expansion of their chief European rivals. It also established a residential trading post staffed by employees of the company. Thus was born the colony of New Netherlands, an economy of fur.

The first two ships of Dutch colonists arrived in 1624, just fifteen years after Hudson's frustrated trip. Unlike Hudson, these colonists came ashore, and stayed ashore as wic employees. Some of them were Walloons – Belgian Huguenots who had come to the Dutch Republic to escape religious persecution – who chose to take free passage, livestock, seeds and other supplies in exchange for six years of unpaid labour on leafy Noten Eyelandt (literally 'Island of Nuts', now Governors Island), just off the coast of Manhattan and the site of the first Dutch colony in North America.

It wasn't long before the New Netherlands' first settlers realized their mistake. Unlike Hudson, they recognized the superior merits of 'Manahatta', the original European transliteration of the Lenape name for the island, and the WIC resettled them there almost immediately, thereby setting a precedent that many New Yorkers cling to today: the supremacy of 'the city' over the 'bridge and tunnel' islands that make up the five boroughs of New York. Manhattan, with its narrow southern tip, was seen as defensible and a natural port of entry to the North American continent. It was an ideal shipping channel, too, since the salt water that flowed into New York Harbor from the Atlantic Ocean kept it from freezing on all but the coldest of winter days. And the rivers that encircled Manhattan were not only rich with cargo possibility but were by every account teeming with salmon, sturgeon, enormous lobsters and the oysters that Hudson's seamen had so admired. The island itself, nearly 34 square miles of forests, pastures and shoreline, promised plenty of room for expansion and a route into New England. It is here that New York can truly be said to have begun, a stone's throw from the paths of Hudson and Verrazzano. The early colonist Adriaen van der Donck noted the colony's

> good opportunities for trade, harbors, waters, fisheries, weather, and wind and many other working appurtenances corresponding with the Netherlands, or in truth and more accurately exceeding the name. So it is for good reason named New Netherland, being as much to say, another or a newfound Netherland.

This 'newfound Netherland' was not in fact new: Native Americans had lived on the Eastern seaboard for centuries, and the Dutch settlement could not but be a major disruption of Native American culture, not to mention daily life. Van der Donck himself learned this lesson early: one of his first assignments in New Netherlands was as a guide and translator between the Dutch and the Lenape, the primary tribe in and around New Amsterdam. The Lenape (the word means 'real people' in the

Algonquian language Unami) were hunters, trappers, fishermen and farmers. They spoke a Munsee dialect of the Algonquin language and made and used wampum – strings or belts of clam- and whelk-shell beads – for ceremonial and exchange purposes. Their cooperation made the New Netherlands' fur trade possible, and there was an active exchange between the *swanneken* or 'people of the sea', as the Lenape called the colonists, and the *wilden*, as some Dutch called the Lenape, who accepted metal goods such as axeheads, pots and firearms for the beaver, otter and mink pelts that they had trapped. The Dutch settlers shipped 1,500 beaver pelts back to Europe in their first year on the island, thanks to this mutually beneficial arrangement. But the harvesting of wild (rather than farmed) animal pelts is hardly sustainable, and the beavers were hunted almost to extinction within a few years. At the same time, the land the Lenape occupied had grown more interesting to the Dutch than their trapping output, and the WIC directed its governors to

> induce [the Lenape] . . . either in return for trading-goods
> or by means of some amicable agreement . . . to give up
> ownership and possession to us, without however forcing
> them thereto in the least or by taking possession by craft
> or fraud, lest we call down the wrath of God upon our
> unrighteous beginnings.

Among the first of these so-called inducements was the purchase of Manhattan itself, an event that has the dubious honour of inspiring New York's first urban legend. The facts are few: a passenger aboard a ship returning to Amsterdam reported to the WIC that Peter Minuit, the third governor of New Netherlands, had 'purchased the Island Manhattes from the Indians for the value of 60 guilder' in 1626. This is the only documentation to suggest that Minuit, who had been requested by his employers to acquire the island, did so in a formal transaction with the Lenape. School textbooks and popular histories commonly hold that Minuit paid Manhattan's 'value' to the Native Americans in a currency of 'beads and trinkets', but this appears to have been the colourful addition of a nineteenth-century American historian. The famous report that the Dutch purchase price is equivalent to U.S.$24 is also a nineteenth-century fable, a calculation based on an 1846 exchange rate for the Dutch guilder – arithmetic that would make a contemporary economist weep. Furthermore, there is significant evidence to suggest that the Native Americans with whom Minuit made his transaction had no cultural basis for understanding the permanence of the arrangement. In Algonquin culture land was not something that one 'owned'. It was a shared resource: one that could be occupied, certainly, by tribes or families who might farm, hunt, or pasture animals there, but hardly a personal possession. Manhattan, they might have argued, belonged to Manhattan.

Unburdened by metaphysical concepts such as these, the Dutch began building in earnest on their new acquisition. Fort Amsterdam was constructed, as well as a stone counting house for the storage of beaver pelts, and a village of *plaggenhutten* (turf houses or sod houses) grew up around it, dubbed 'Nieuw Amsterdam' or New Amsterdam, in honour of the Dutch Republic's chief port city and the headquarters of the Dutch West India Company. It was a company town at first, occupied by artisans, farmers and builders as well as the people who make their livings from them: clerks, accountants and soldiers. But the WIC soon found its long-distance employees hard to manage, for a number of reasons. Coopers, masons, bakers and other entrepreneurs were hampered by the commercial monopoly of the WIC, which regulated their production and limited their distribution to keep the economic climate favourable to the products of the motherland. Manhattan's farmers, on the other hand, discouraged by poor soil, limited livestock and the threat of Lenape raids, were soon lured into the more lucrative business of trapping for fur. To maintain control, the company took a number of steps to ameliorate economic conditions on the ground and to placate the colonists with amenities imported from the Dutch Republic. They decentralized ownership by making tracts of land north and west of Manhattan available for investment by major stockholders, wealthy Dutch landlords called *patroons*. They recruited immigrants from northern and western Europe to the colony's labour force and, beginning in 1626, underwrote the purchase of African (and later West Indian) slaves for the same purpose. They imported a *ziekentrooster*, or 'comforter of the sick', and a schoolmaster for the colony's children. They established a branch of the Reform Dutch Church inside Fort Amsterdam and advertised freedom of conscience for all colonists (although the freedom to worship in public was only guaranteed to Reform congregants). They expanded New Netherlands into the contemporary boroughs of Brooklyn, Queens, Staten Island and the Bronx, distributing land grants to ambitious farmers, and appointed increasingly hands-on governors to shape the growing, diverse and unruly population that the company had encouraged in the first place.

The first attempt at strong leadership was an unmitigated disaster. It took the form of Governor Willem Kieft, a Dutch merchant who arrived in New Amsterdam in 1638 and was sent home in disgrace nine years later. While Kieft is credited with founding the city's first legislative body, known as the Council of Twelve Men, he chose, paradoxically, to overrule every decision handed down by it. His most calamitous actions involved the Lenape, on whom he levied an involuntary tax to defray the cost of building and munitioning neighbouring Dutch forts (which could presumably be used against a Native American attack). The Lenape's refusal to pay and Kieft's subsequent retribution led to five years of outright war between the Dutch settlers and the Raritan, Hackensack and Weckquaesgeek tribes. Among the most atrocious events of what has become known as Kieft's War was the gruesome massacre of at least 120 Tappan and Weckquaesgeek people who had fled from Mohawk incursions to makeshift refugee camps at what is now Jersey City, New Jersey and at Corlears Hook, a promontory on the edge of what is today the Lower East Side. Men, women and children were killed with abandon, with the Dutch reportedly throwing children into the icy river waters and shooting the parents who attempted to rescue them. While Kieft's tenure did not mark the last time that the Dutch would take up arms against their Native American neighbours, it is generally regarded as the most brutal and egregious episode in New Amsterdam's short history.

It is surprising and a little gratifying to a contemporary New Yorker to find that the WIC did, as they had warned, frown on the bloodthirsty government of Willem Kieft, recalling him to the Netherlands in response to the demands of the colonists. The ship carrying the disgraced governor sank on the way there, but the dramatic end to Kieft's tenure was quickly

A stained-glass portrait of New Amsterdam's last governor, Peter Stuyvesant, in St Mark's Church in-the-Bowery, where he is buried.

forgotten in the stir caused by his successor. The next and final governor of New Netherlands is certainly the best known today: Peter Stuyvesant, the domineering, peg-legged warrior who brought a measure of order and infrastructure to the unruly colony. By the time Stuyvesant arrived in 1647, New Amsterdam was already a diverse, polyglot hub where no fewer than eighteen languages were spoken and the WIC's trade monopoly had given way to a free market. It was becoming a city of some self-government, too: a court of *burgemeesters* and *schepenen* (aldermen) was established in 1653, while several villages, including Breuckelen (later Brooklyn), had their own sitting justices. But Stuyvesant, like some more recent New York mayors, had no interest in being ruled entirely by the people, even if the people were burgomasters. The list of his laws, regulations and municipal reforms affords a window into New Amsterdam's rapid growth and Stuyvesant's anxiety to direct – if not entirely check – the beginnings of a physical and social urban sprawl. They also illustrate the contradictions inherent in the very idea of colonial freedom. Stuyvesant sought to control sales of alcoholic beverages and made Sunday church observance mandatory. He built a 12-foot wall to protect the colony (on the site of Wall Street) and opened Breede Weg, now known as Broadway. He prohibited reckless driving within the city limits and improved fencing laws to curb wandering (and destructive) livestock. He instituted fire laws and built New Amsterdam's first pier, opened free grammar schools and imported schoolmasters by the dozen. A slaveowner himself, he ruled that the colony's 'half-free' slaves, those who had worked off their enslavement to the WIC over a period of years, could own indentured servants and intermarry (provided they were Reform Protestants). He forbade the sale of liquor – and, curiously, of Dutch cookies – to the Native Americans. Some of these decrees (such as the last one) were met with derision by the citizens of New Amsterdam, but others helped to further the shaping of the little colonial hub into a metropolis with global aspirations.

It was not, however, a locus of universal tolerance, as many contemporary New Yorkers like to assert. On the contrary,

The storefront of the former Vesuvio Bakery, founded on Prince Street in SoHo in 1920. The Birdbath Bakery currently occupies the space, but retains the original awning and signage.

BAKING FOR THE 'WILDEN'

Peter Stuyvesant never instituted a ban on smoking or on trans fats, as former New York mayor Michael Bloomberg did, but according to the historian Jaap Jacobs, the Dutch director general did heavily regulate the colony's brewing and baking industries. In particular, he took measures to prevent the bakers of the New Netherlands colony from 'baking white bread, *krakelingen* and cookies for the Indians rather than the normal rye bread for the colonists'. Wheat and rye were precious commodities in New Netherlands, and the government was concerned that bakers were squandering their store in baking luxuries to sell at a high price to their Native American trading partners, rather than in supplying the daily needs of the Dutch (a less profitable enterprise).

To add insult to delicious injury, many bakers were enriching the bread they sold illegally with other luxury ingredients, such as sugar, currants and prunes. Stuyvesant instituted a ban: any baker found making sweet treats for the *'wilde en barberissche naturellen'* (wild and barbarous natives) was to be fined 50 guilders.

Stuyvesant's government was constantly being reproached by the WIC for acts of bigotry that were out of keeping with the company's business-friendly image: they had no interest in turning away any group that could make a profit for New Netherlands. To this end, they insisted that Stuyvesant accept a boat carrying 23 Jewish refugees from Recife, Brazil, who had petitioned the Dutch Republic for permission to land in New York after being rejected by Stuyvesant's authorities. Stuyvesant did so grudgingly, and then immediately put in place laws that restricted the Jewish settlers' ability to obtain sacred spaces for worship or burial grounds, to practice trades or to keep shop. It must be noted that the governor's religious prejudice was remarkably even-handed: he also caused a number of Quakers to be arrested and exiled on grounds of illegal public worship, thus precipitating the Flushing Remonstrance, a document that is widely recognized as the first North American petition for universal religious tolerance. The eloquent Remonstrance, which was signed in 1657 by Quakers and English citizens of 'Vlishing' (now Flushing, Queens), left Stuyvesant unmoved, but after he forcibly banished the English Quaker John Bowne to Holland, the WIC intervened: 'You may therefore shut your eyes, at least not force people's consciences, but allow everyone to have his own belief, as long as he behaves quietly and legally.' This precept did not, apparently, apply to the Native Americans, with whom Stuyvesant's government had a protracted exchange of hostilities over the capture and recapture of New Sweden (Delaware), a Swedish outpost with ties to the Susquehannock tribe. The battles ended in the sacking of Staten Island and the ransoming of more than 150 white hostages who had been taken by the Susquehannock.

Setting aside the fight for land and civil liberties, there is no mistaking Peter Stuyvesant's New Amsterdam for New York. As seen in the 'Castello Plan', a 1660 map of the colony by cartographer Jacques Cortelyou, New Amsterdam was still essentially a trading post, with Fort Amsterdam as its southernmost anchor and focal point. The city, the ancient map reveals, was touchingly miniaturized: beyond the

settlement's northernmost 'Land-Gate' at what is now
Rector Street, the tiny city's orderly (if somewhat misshapen)
crosshatch of named streets (Beaver, Prince, Market, High)
quickly dissolved into an assortment of unmarked roads
leading to privately owned 'bouweries', tobacco plantations,
warehouses, ferry landings and grain mills. North of these
properties was forested land, with 'suburban' or 'summer'
communities to be found in 'New Haarlem', near Manhattan's
upper shores. Breede Weg, the street that would become
Broadway, is visible on the Castello Plan, running up the
island like a crooked spine. Even at this early date it was already
a shapeshifter of a street, reflecting the diverse communities it
serves. Broadway began as a Weckquaesgeek hunting trail, and
in 1660 it still served this purpose at its northernmost point,
hard by the narrow strait now called the Harlem River. The

The cemetery of the Dutch Reformed Church in Flatbush, Brooklyn.
The church congregation dates to 1654, and the oldest (legible) tombstone
was laid before the Revolutionary War.

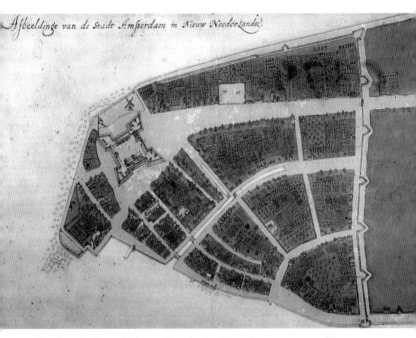

Afbeeldinge van de Stadt Amsterdam in Nieuw Neederlandt.

The Castello Plan, widely considered to be the earliest extant map of New Amsterdam, 1660.

road widened as it moved south, finally ending inside the city walls as a smooth, even sophisticated dirt thoroughfare for horses and wagons on their way to New Amsterdam's busy harbour. From the perspective of the Castello Plan, the Dutch hold on the island of Manhattan seemed very fragile indeed. And so it proved for Stuyvesant and his citizens, who were the last to discover, in 1664, that Charles II of England had given New Netherlands to his brother James, the Duke of York, without any thought as to the prior Dutch claim on the colony. The duke, as eager to move in as any New Yorker possessed of luxury real estate, sent four warships to Gravesend Bay in Brooklyn, along with a letter to Stuyvesant demanding his capitulation. The governor, pressured by his constituents, surrendered, bringing 40 years of Dutch rule to an end – at least for a time.

Although the colony of New York had been easily won, the English did not take it for granted. Manhattan, in particular, struck its conquerors as a kind of primitive paradise. 'If there be any terrestrial Canaans, 'tis surely here,' rhapsodized Daniel Denton in a letter sent home to England in 1670, 'where all the Land floweth with milk & Honey. The inhabitants are blest with Peace & plenty, blessed in their Countrey, blessed in their Fields, blessed in the Fruit of their bodies, [and] in the fruit of their grounds.' How best to increase the quantity of 'milk and honey' provided by the new New York was now the task of the colony's English governors, the earliest of whom took a relatively laissez-faire approach to their new domain, perhaps because their individual tenures were often very short. Between 1664 and 1673, the city had three mayors and played host to two provincial governors whose municipal improvements were limited to numerous intercolonial customs duties and a new legal code that made sodomy a capital offence and lacked any provision for public assembly or public education. In defence of these conscriptees of the king, their efforts were cut short in 1673 by an unexpected coup. Taking advantage of the Third Anglo-Dutch War, 23 Dutch ships arrived in New York Harbor and sent word that they had arrived to retake what 'was theyr own, and theyr own would they have'. When the English balked at having their strategy thrown back at them, and demanded to see the sailors' royal commission, they were told that it was in the barrel of a cannon and would be delivered soon. After a brief skirmish, the English surrendered. On 30 July 1673 New York was again New Amsterdam, but too late for its last governor – Peter Stuyvesant had died at his 'Bouwerie'

Garden view of St Marks Church in-the-Bowery, once the family seat of the Stuyvesants.

home the year before. In any case, the Dutch recapture lasted for little more than a year before England and the Netherlands came to mutually agreeable terms and the colony was returned to its once and future master.

It is possible that the unexpected interregnum of 1673 galvanized the English to make something out of this hard-won prize, or that the city's governors finally had time enough to implement improvements and Anglicizations that had been planned all along. At any rate, New Yorkers began to see changes: an intercolonial post began, carrying mail to Hartford and Boston; the city's first commercial wharf, merchant's exchange and insane asylum were built; and ordinances requiring street lanterns and cobblestones to be installed were issued. While Dutch citizens were still allowed to speak and worship in their native language, major New York landmarks were soon translated: Fort Amsterdam became Fort James, Heeren Gracht was dubbed Broad Street and new streets (including the first street opened by the English, which they actually called 'New Street') were christened with monarchical names such as Crown Street or Little Queen Street. At first, the English attempted to govern their busy province from afar, only to decide that granting the wealthy landowners of Manhattan and Long Island a representative assembly was easier than facing an incipient taxpayer rebellion. It is meaningful that the 'Charter of Liberties and Privileges' that resulted from this early decision in 1683 included not only representative government, trial by jury and protections against martial law, but provisions for religious toleration that are broader than any agreed to by Peter Stuyvesant. The Dutch are universally given credit for creating the conditions under which diversity could thrive in New York, but it was the English who actually codified and protected that diversity.

Despite this charter and the freedoms it afforded, a second overthrow of the English government took place in New York just five years later, after the ascendance in 1685 of the Catholic James ii, formerly the Duke of York, to the throne. James began by formally disallowing the region's brand-new charter and its provisions for self-government, but scarcely had time to do more before he himself was swept out of power by the Glorious Revolution of 1688, which brought the Protestant and Dutch king Willem of Orange to the English, Scottish and Irish thrones. New Yorkers, galvanized by this news, made a power play for the colony, seizing Fort James and banishing all English officials from the region. In the midst of the resulting chaos, a German-born militia captain emerged as chief military commander of all the New York counties except Albany: Jacob Leisler, a fervent enemy of Catholicism and zealous defender of Willem of Orange. Taking advantage of the months of travel time necessary for Willem's appointed governor to arrive, Leisler appointed himself New York's 'lieutenant governor' in the interim. For two years, Leisler ruled southern New York, collecting taxes from his fellow New Yorkers and defending New York's borders from French and Native American incursions with his militia (with mixed results). Leisler also allowed the citizens of Manhattan to choose their own mayor in a vote, the last time that would take place for more than 100 years. This kind of total political upset seems far-fetched today, but as the capture and recapture of New Amsterdam from the Dutch suggests, the English grip on the colony was just as tenuous as Stuyvesant's had proved to be, and the diversity of industries, interests and ethnic groups that had made New York so attractive also made it a challenge to control. When the king's chosen representatives finally did arrive, Leisler refused to cede the government or the fort, and six weeks of standoffs and skirmishes ensued, splitting the city into pro- and anti-Leisler factions. While most of Leisler's supporters were ultimately pardoned, he and his military commander were executed on charges of treason. Leisler's tenure was brief and badly executed, by all accounts, but it was also illustrative: his temporary coup was proof that the merchants and artisans of New York could band together in a common cause, even if, as Theodore Roosevelt pointed out in his history of New York, it would be nearly a century before that cause was 'democratic government and manhood suffrage' rather than 'foreign monarchy [and] native oligarchy'.

Interestingly, it was under the 'Dutch' Willem of Orange that New York truly became an English colony. The Church of England was established as the official church of New York, Queens, Richmond and Westchester counties in 1693, and Trinity Church was erected as its urban anchor at the corner of Broadway and Wall Street in Manhattan. Dutch walls and canals in the city were demolished, and Dutch weights and measures was abandoned in favour of the English system. New Yorkers were forbidden from exporting directly to the independent nations of Scotland and Ireland and, to ensure that they did not compete with the mother country, from exporting any woollen items whatsoever – anywhere.

At the same time that New York was becoming more English, it was also becoming more sophisticated. The first coffeehouse in the city opened in the early eighteenth century, as did the first bar association, the first public school and, crucially, the first public printing press. The city also manufactured its first celebrities at this time, chiefly Captain William Kidd and New York's fourteenth governor, Edward Hyde, Viscount Cornbury. Captain Kidd is better known to posterity as a dashing, if murderous, pirate, but the Scottish-born sea captain began as one of New York's chief protectors, famous for having run off enemy privateers from the city's coastline. From 1690 to 1695 Kidd was a churchgoing member of the colony's upper class and lived in considerable luxury with his twice-widowed wife at the corner of Pearl Street and Hanover Square. Six years later, he would be hanged at London's Execution Dock for multiple counts of murder and piracy. Lord Cornbury, in contrast, appears to have been tabloid-worthy from the start. He was accused, among other things, of forgery, bribery and embezzlement of public funds: in one instance he appropriated monies collected to build batteries at the [Verrazzano] Narrows in order to build himself a country home on Governors Island, and then lied to the Common Council about his action. More surprising, perhaps, was the rumour of his penchant for cross-dressing, which has never been proven to the satisfaction of historians.

Regardless of Lord Cornbury's sartorial preferences, he was removed from office by England's Queen Anne in 1708, whereupon New York's Common Council put him in prison until he could repay his substantial debts (and leave the country for good). The international scandals of Kidd and Cornbury did more than titillate New Yorkers: they served as proof of the colony's nascent cosmopolitanism at the turn of a new century. By the mid-eighteenth century New York had grown into a place of real consequence, one with a circulating library, a university, a growing roster of newspapers, a theatre and an intellectual community, not to mention a diversity of houses of worship that surpassed even London. Visitors marvelled at the city's elegant homes and well-dressed gentry, and noted their fondness for good food and spirited entertainment, including 'turtle feasts' at country taverns in 'Bloomingdale' on what is now the Upper East Side. At the same time, New Yorkers were also beginning to acquire their reputation for being fast-talking and uncouth: often less refined than they seemed at first glance. Visiting from Boston, the future president John Adams lamented:

> with all the opulence and splendor of this city, there is very little good breeding to be found. [New Yorkers] talk very loud, very fast, and altogether. If they ask you a question, before you can utter three words of your answer, they will break out upon you again and talk away.

Another Bostonian, Sarah Knight, concerned herself with the state of New Yorkers' souls, reporting: '[They are] not as strict in keeping the Sabbath as in Boston and other places.' It was to this less genteel New York that some of its more infamous colonial institutions belonged: a thriving slave market and a famous red-light district, located hard by Trinity Church and known as the 'Holy Ground'.

The population that supported these urban developments had nearly doubled from 1700 to 1750, when it stood at 37,000 (with about 40 per cent of households owning slaves). It had been subject to epidemics of smallpox and yellow fever as well as several slave revolts that ended in bloody reprisals. In the most brutal episode, referred to in contemporary literature as the 'Great Negro Plot of 1741', 30 slaves were executed – many burned at the stake or hanged from a gibbet until their lifeless bodies decomposed completely; 71 were banished and 154 jailed for taking part in a supposed 'conspiracy' to burn down the city, all on the testimony of one white woman.

The story of this alleged revolt and its horrific consequences throws another trial into stark relief: that of John Peter Zenger, a printer and newspaper publisher whose *New York Weekly Journal* was the most outspoken advocate for freedom of the press in the colony. In the early 1730s Zenger began publishing essays in the *Weekly Journal* that were critical of New York's government (and, by extension, of George II, the current monarch) and questioned the arbitrary decisions being made by the provincial governor, William Cosby, in his dealings with the Common Council and its magistrates. 'To Conclude: Power without Control appertains to God alone; and no Man ought to be trusted with what no Man is equal to,' the printer wrote in one editorial in 1733. Charged by an angry Cosby with seditious libel, he was thrown into prison and would likely have remained there until his death had his cause not been taken up by a lawyer named Andrew Hamilton, who argued before a New York jury that a statement could not be libellous if it were true. 'As we well know,' Hamilton argued,

> it is not two centuries ago that a man would have been burned at the stake for owning such opinions in matters of religion as are publicly written and printed at this day . . . I think it is pretty clear that in New York a man may make very free with his God, but he must take special care what he says of the Governor.

Zenger was acquitted, but not before Hamilton seized the chance to make the case for self-government, saying:

> It is not the cause of a poor printer, nor of New York alone, which you are now trying. No! It may in its consequences

An 18th-century portrait of a lady that has been rumoured to be 'the second Earl of Clarendon in Women's cloaths'.

LORD CORNBURY'S CLOTHES

'I must say something [which] perhaps no boddy [sic] will think worth their while to tell,' a colonist wrote in a formal complaint against Edward Hyde, Viscount Cornbury, 'and that is, his dressing publicly in woman's cloaths every day, and putting a stop to all publique business while he is pleaseing himselfe with [that] peculiar but detestable magot [grotesque behaviour].' Another colonist wrote on the same theme, if with less shock: 'My Lord Cornbury has and dos still make use of an unfortunate Custom of dressing himself in Womens Cloaths and of exposing himself in that Garb upon the Ramparts to the view of the public; in that dress he draws a World of Spectators about him and consequently as many Censures.' Was the fourteenth English governor of New York a cross-dresser? Historians say it isn't likely, but scandals, even 300-year-old scandals, have impressive staying power.

Lord Cornbury's reputation for drag is based on just a handful of letters written by New Yorkers who fiercely opposed his government, as well as on the posthumous cataloguing of a full-length portrait of a woman with masculine features as 'the second Earl of Clarendon in Women's cloaths'. This portrait was purchased by the New-York Historical Society in 1952 and hangs in their galleries. Never mind that Cornbury was himself, as historian Patricia Bonomi has pointed out, the third earl, not the second.

The supposed evidence of the letters and the existence of the image – however inaccurately catalogued – has proved sufficient to maintain his fame to the present day. The New-York Historical Society, while distancing themselves from the 'popular legend' of Cornbury's cross-dressing, still sells reproductions of the portrait in their gift shop. In the twenty-first century, the possibility of a transvestite colonial governor only reinforces New Yorkers' sense of their own exceptionalism and eccentricity.

affect every freeman that lives under a British government on the main of America. It is the best cause. It is the cause of liberty.

Hamilton's remarks won him a formal resolution of thanks from New York's Common Council, and published accounts of Zenger's trial and Hamilton's impassioned argument sold briskly on both sides of the Atlantic. The lawyer's language of liberty would resonate with New Yorkers in the coming decades, and seemed particularly prescient when the British Parliament handed down the Stamp Act just three decades later. This Act of 1765 was a tax on the paper used for official printed media, such as newspapers and legal documents, in the Thirteen Colonies. Unlike most previous taxes, it was both direct and involuntary: the colonial legislatures had been offered no vote or veto. The purpose of the tax was to defray the cost of maintaining British soldiers in North America after the French and Indian War (the North American theatre of the Seven Years War, 1754–63), but it turned out to create its own kind of firepower. Galvanized by this perceived injustice, colonists from Massachusetts down to North Carolina rallied to convene a Stamp Act Congress in New York. The Congress, which is generally considered the first joint assembly of the American colonies, drew up a Declaration of Rights and Grievances that protested against the unconstitutionality of the Act and insisted on the colonists' rights as British subjects. Such a document may be seen as a predecessor to the founding documents of the United States of America, although the Declaration of Rights and Grievances does make a point of pledging the delegates' loyalty to George III. The choice of New York City as the crucible for such a document is surprising, considering the city's history as a place founded on the principles of commerce rather than of conscience. Ultimately, however, it was commerce that forced Britain's hand after more than 200 New York merchants signed an agreement to cease all trade with the motherland. The impact of this embargo on the British economy was too significant to ignore, and Parliament repealed the Act the very next year.

New Yorkers celebrated the birthday of George III and the repeal simultaneously, and the blended festivities neatly illustrate the mixed sympathies of the largely Tory city.

This is not to suggest that the Stamp Act did not have a catalytic effect on many New Yorkers. The New York chapter of the Sons of Liberty, an underground organization of civilians with the motto 'no taxation without representation', skirmished with British soldiers over the course of two days in January 1770. This early encounter, dubbed the Battle of Golden Hill, marks the first bloodshed of the Revolution – it preceded the more famous Boston Massacre by six weeks. Meanwhile, business owners in the city protested every fresh effort to tax imports, crippling British trade with their unofficial embargoes. At the same time, the city continued to add to its list of firsts: the first university (King's College, later Columbia University), hard by the infamous Holy Ground, first medical school, first hospital, first chamber of commerce. Increasingly New Yorkers had no need to import from overseas: colonial artisans in the greater metropolitan area could provide everything from fine linen to fire engines. Nor did they need to import soldiers: the second Quartering Act of 1774, drawn up in the wake of the Boston Tea Party, ensured that British redcoats could occupy every empty barn, mill, inn or other privately owned, non-residential space in the city. It would not be New York's last occupation.

3 A Post of Infinite Importance

New Yorkers declared their independence from Britain by beheading the king. On 9 July 1776 a gilded, life-sized statue of George III on horseback that the British had placed at Bowling Green in 1770 was toppled by patriot troops, who severed the head of the monarch and stripped the gilt from the dissected figures (both horse and rider), the better to make use of the 4,000 pounds of lead that lay beneath. 'The Lead we hear Is to be run up into musket balls for the use of the Yankees,' Lieutenant Isaac Bangs wrote in his journal, 'when it is hoped that the emanations of the Leaden George will make as deep impressions in the Bodies of some of his red coated and Torie Subjects.' The very next day, the provincial convention at White Plains resolved 'that the style or title of this House be changed from that of "the Provincial Congress of the Colony of New-York" to that of "the Convention of the Representatives of the State of New-York"'. Two days later, the Declaration of Independence was first published in a New York newspaper, and Admiral Richard Howe, who had filled New York's harbour with an armada of more than 400 British ships (the largest naval force ever to reach American shores) opened fire on rebel batteries on both sides of the Hudson. It was a dramatic entrance into the war in which New York would play an integral role, and a longer one than anyone could have imagined.

Both redcoats and rebels could agree on one thing: New York was not another Boston. Politically it was hardly a hotbed of resistance like that New England city. Hearts and minds were divided in many wards on Manhattan, which had reached a population of 20,000 by the beginning of the

Die Zerstörung der Königlichen Bild | La Destruction de la Statuë royale
Saule zu Neu Yorck. | a Nouvelle York

Rather than showing the toppling of the equestrian statue of George III by troops, this misguided attempt by the artist in fact shows the pulling down of a statue of a standing man, by a group who seem to be mainly slaves.

war. The piecemeal American army, assembled from individual colonial regiments and lacking an official uniform or a flag, seemed out of place in fashionable New York, so much so that it was routinely called 'The New England Army' rather than the 'Continental' or 'American' army. So, too, did General George Washington, a gentleman farmer who seems to have had difficulty finding real estate in Manhattan that was large enough for his Virginia-sized retinue: in search of a comfortable berth, the general and his family headquartered in many of the grandest mansions at both ends of the island, making it possible for more than a handful of New York spaces to legitimately claim to the present day that 'George Washington slept here'. It was true that the Provincial Congress of the colonies had its beginnings in Manhattan, but the delegates, including New York patriarch John Jay, had already beat a hasty retreat northward to Kingston. At the start of the war a majority of the property in New York City still belonged to Tories, and more than half of the city's business owners were avowed loyalists. Beyond Manhattan, Tory support was even stronger: Staten and Long Islands, in particular, had been settled by

English colonists and remained bastions of British sympathy, home to citizen militias preparing for the chance to aid the king's cause. While this portrait of political dubiety might suggest that the former colony was a less than worthy wartime prize, it was in fact the opposite. New York, John Adams admitted that year, was 'a kind of key to the whole continent'. The 11-mile island was the key for both sides, for the very reason that Admiral Howe had already illustrated with his armada in July 1776: the Hudson River was the gateway to the northern corridor, the best passage to Canada and the fastest way to cut Boston itself off from the rest of the colonies. Narrow little Manhattan, with its admirable harbour and ambivalent citizens, must be defended at all costs.

Key or no key, many of New York's citizens had already decided to forsake their city. By the summer of 1776, one-third of New Yorkers, both Tories and patriots, had fled lower Manhattan. By mid-August General Washington had issued a general recommendation that all women, children and 'infirm Persons' be removed from Manhattan immediately, 'trusting', he added, 'that with the Blessing of Heaven, upon the American Arms, they may soon return to it in perfect Security'. Removal from the city meant moving north towards Bloomingdale, or out of state altogether, to patriot-controlled New Jersey or Connecticut. It would prove to be a much longer rustication than any New Yorker, Tory or patriot, could have anticipated. For those who stayed, the city was a place of factions and fear: patriot mobs routinely routed prominent Tories out of their homes to subject them to a host of grisly public humiliations (including tarring and feathering), while fusillades from the British fleet massed in the harbour sent cannonballs bouncing through the gardens and walls of homes close to the shore. Beyond Manhattan, British and Hessian (German mercenary) regiments had mobilized to cover Staten Island with 32,000 troops – more than the population of Philadelphia, the largest colonial city at the time. The war had begun in earnest.

The story of New York as a site of military action during the Revolutionary War is a tale more of disappointment than daring: some of the most spectacular tactical failures of the war happened in greater New York, before the Continental Army had a chance to cohere as a unified fighting force. The first engagement – and the first failure – came to be known as the Battle of Brooklyn (or the Battle of Long Island) and took place on 27 August 1776, just ten days after Washington's call for the civilian evacuation of Manhattan. Forty thousand troops took part in a day-long offensive that ranged over the hilly farms and pastures of South Brooklyn, where the residential neighbourhoods of Brooklyn Heights, Cobble Hill, Fort Greene and Red Hook can be found today. The patriots, whose ranks had been weakened by dysentery and smallpox, were outnumbered nearly three to one by the redcoats. The battle was, as one American soldier deemed it, a 'severe flogging' for the patriots, many of whom were killed or taken prisoner by the British. Washington's forces were not entirely routed, however: a day later the remaining American army – some 9,000 soldiers – were safely ferried across the East River to Manhattan under cover of darkness and serendipitous fog, to the surprise and dismay of their pursuers, who followed

Triumphal entrance of royal troops in New York.

The retreat of the First Maryland Regiment, the Battle of Brooklyn, 1776.

them north to Harlem and Washington Heights, where a devastating rout at Fort Washington made the British occupation of Manhattan official.

The Battle of Brooklyn would prove to be the first of many opportunities the British would have to amass prisoners in New York, and their treatment of captured soldiers remains one of the flashpoints of Revolutionary War histories to this day. The British interned their prisoners on board ships that they docked in Wallabout Bay, between Brooklyn and the East side of Manhattan Island (the better to prevent escapes), and in privately owned sugar houses commandeered after

Washington's evacuation. Whether on land or sea, these prisons were reported by both sides to be living charnel pits, crowded with mostly naked, starving and diseased soldiers who were crowded, neglected and given little access to fresh water or fresh air, let alone clothing, food or medical treatment. 'We have now got near 5,000 prisoners in New-York,' a British correspondent wrote to the *London Packet* in 1777, 'and many of them are such ragamuffins, as you never saw in your life: I cannot give you a better Idea of them than by putting you in mind of Falstaff's recruits, or poor Tom in King Lear; and yet they had strained every nerve to cover their Nakedness.' Captain Alexander Coffin Jr, an American naval officer detained on the prison-ship *Jersey*, wrote about the provision boat that came daily to bring supplies from Manhattan to the captives floating on Wallabout Bay, a boat named *The Relief*: 'In fact,' he wrote, 'the said schooner might emphatically be termed the *Relief*, for the execrable water and provisions she carried *relieved* many of my brave but unfortunate countrymen by death, from the misery and savage treatment they daily endured.' When soldiers on the floating prisons died, they were routinely thrown into the East River, and their bones would wash up on the western shore of Brooklyn for decades to come.

The prison ships are an enduring image of wartime New York in part because they were parked in the harbour for so long: Manhattan was occupied by the British for a total of seven years. It is not hard to see why Britain would have chosen to make New York City her wartime headquarters: although small compared to London, the pre-Revolutionary city was sophisticated out of all proportion to its size. Those billeted there during the war reported that the city was 'one of the prettiest, pleasantest harbor towns [to be] seen . . . [with] houses . . . built fine and regular in English style'. But the war obliterated much of what made the city so charming to visitors, as did the Great Fire of 1776, which arrived in Manhattan four days after Admiral Howe. The fire, which is thought to have started in a tavern, left a devastating scar that ran up the west side of the city, from Whitehall Slip to Barclay Street. Before the conflagration could be contained,

Monument to the Prison Ship Martyrs in Fort Greene Park, Brooklyn.

The fire of 1776.

provision the British army, forced to billet soldiers in their
homes and hemmed in with regulations on their own
enterprise. As the years of occupation wore on, it seemed
increasingly impossible – particularly from the vantage point
of New York City – that Washington's ragged troops could
prevail, even after they garnered the support and firepower of
the French and Spanish governments. The appointed colonial
governor of New York went so far as to re-establish civil
government on Staten and Long Islands in anticipation
of victory. 'I have the pleasure to acquaint you', one British
officer wrote to the London paper *Lloyd's Evening Post* in 1781,

> that our affairs go on so extremely well, that I doubt
> not but we shall soon be Masters of all America, for it is
> impossible for them to hold out much longer; Washington's
> army is reduced to a handful of men . . . [while] this city
> [New York] is crowded with inhabitants who come from
> all parts of America, to be out of the hands of the arbitrary
> Congress, who are become odious to the greatest part of
> the people.

Less than seven months later, the British lieutenant general
Lord Cornwallis would surrender to Washington and the
French Comte de Rochambeau at Yorktown, Virginia, and

the Revolutionary War came to an end. On the morning of 25 November, the war ended in New York City, too: a squad led by the patriot General Henry Knox marched from northern Manhattan to the Bowery and met up with General Washington and Governor Clinton near the Battery for a victory parade that lasted for a week, culminating in spectacular fireworks and a New York tradition: the celebration of 'Evacuation Day' would endure for the next century.

But the actual evacuation day was a bit of a misnomer: in fact, it took two years for the British to exit New York City after their formal capitulation. In addition to 10,000 garrisoned British soldiers, a staggering 35,000 loyalists from across the thirteen colonies had sought asylum in New York, and had to be repatriated safely or risk violence, ignominy and bankruptcy in the United States. This number included more than 2,000 freed or runaway slaves who had been promised emancipation by the British in exchange for loyalty. While neither Britain nor the colonies would achieve full manumission of slavery for decades to come, many formerly enslaved colonists preferred to start new lives elsewhere. For many loyalists, 'elsewhere' was Nova Scotia, which accepted 30,000 former colonists, while a total of 2,500 ended up in the Bahamas. It was, as the historian Maya Jasanoff suggests, the 'largest civilian transfer' in the history of the United States.

Once they had recovered from the week-long party, New Yorkers set about reclaiming their city. It seemed like a national effort at first: Manhattan, which had been the hub of enemy activity, was now the new nation's first capital. General Washington was sworn in as the nation's first president from the steps of the city's sparkling new Federal Hall, on the corner of Wall and Nassau Streets. The first Congress met in New York, where they drafted the Bill of Rights and the Judiciary Act that set up the federal court system. Thus established as the centre of the new American universe, the city celebrated that fact by launching municipal improve- ments at lightning speed. These include the founding of the Bank of New York by Alexander Hamilton; the creation of the New York Board of Regents to ensure standards across

Stone Street (formerly Duke Street), one of the colonial, cobblestoned streets of lower Manhattan, as it looks today.

STREET NAMES

After the Revolutionary War, New Yorkers turned to the task of renaming their city. Not the metropolis itself, however, but many of its colonial streets (those in today's lower Manhattan), which had been given a royal flavour by more than 100 years of English rule. Trees and flowers replaced many monarchical monikers: Little Queen Street became Cedar Street, King Street was changed to Pine Street and Prince Street became Rose Street. Still other rechristenings had more patriotic associations: in 1794, Crown Street was changed to Liberty Street, for obvious reasons.

These renamings were more gradual and less thorough than might be expected after a republican victory: Little George Street (now Spruce Street) and Duke Street (now Stone Street) can be found on the 1807 Kirkham Map of New York City, while other names with decidedly English import (Hanover Square, York Street, Fletcher Street) still exist today. Dutch street names — such as Cortland and Nassau Streets, Maiden Lane and Coenties Slip — were mostly exempted from this housecleaning, perhaps because they honoured New York residents rather than their rulers, or because they represented a colonial past seen through rose-coloured glasses. Interestingly, some of the streets that seem most likely to be honouring an English monarch (Elizabeth, William, James and Ann) were in fact named after the Dutch and English landowners and merchants who settled those respective neighbourhoods.

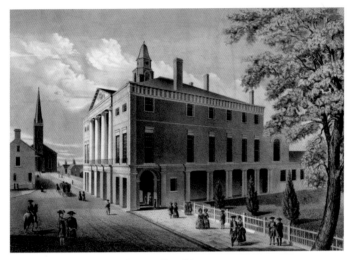

Federal Hall, Wall Street and Trinity Church in 1789.

public and private schools; the reopening of King's College (now called Columbia College); the organization of insurance companies and the establishment of a u.s. Customs Service by Congress. In an effort to erase the memory of occupation fully, the New York Common Council began rechristening the city's crooked colonial streets with staunchly republican names: George Street became Spruce Street, King Street was dubbed Pine Street and Little Queen Street was baptized Cedar Street. Social improvements were put in place by New York residents as well: the Manumission Society was founded in 1784 to provide aid to freed slaves, as was the Friendly Sons of St Patrick, a charity to support Irish immigrants. The Society of St Tammany, the most powerful fraternal organization in the history of New York City, was also created during this period, to lasting effect, as was the Friendly Club, the city's first literary society. Entertainments flourished, too: at the John Street Theatre, the American Company was performing the first American play, Royall Tyler's *The Contrast* (written in the style of English playwright Richard Brinsley Sheridan's famous comedy of manners *The School for Scandal*), and *Charlotte Temple: A Tale of Truth*, a melodramatic, 'true' account of a young woman betrayed by a dastardly British soldier, became the new nation's first best-selling novel.

'In point of sociability and hospitality,' a visiting Noah Webster wrote in 1788, 'New York is hardly exceeded by any town in the United States.' But despite this lively reputation, and the municipal and cultural advances mentioned above, the city was unable to retain the seat of the federal government for more than two years. In 1790, Congress decamped for Philadelphia, a wealthy city of tidy squares and Franklinian innovation that a recent English visitor had described as 'the object of everyone's wonder and admiration'. The removal was a temporary measure in anticipation of the completion of the Capitol building in the District of Columbia, but it was seen as a short-term improvement, too: Philadelphia had been occupied by the British for one year, as opposed to New York's seven, and thus had a head start in matters of population, commerce and general refinement. It was also not 'a pigsty', as Representative Fisher Ames of Massachusetts referred to Manhattan. But not everyone was happy with Congress's decision. 'And, when all is done, it will not be Broadway,' Abigail Adams complained about her future home in the City of Brotherly Love. What was it about busy, dirty Broadway that she found so ineffably compelling? In a few years, New Yorkers would have the vocabulary to tell her.

On the 200th anniversary of Hudson's discovery, the New-York Historical Society issued an impassioned plea in the form of a public notice to the citizens of New York:

> Do you know anything respecting the first settlement of New-York by the Dutch; the number of the settlers; the time of their arrival, their general character . . . Can you give any information which will throw light on the state of morals in our country, at different periods, such as the comparative frequency of drunkenness, gambling, duelling, suicide, conjugal infidelity, prostitution, &c. &c.?

This clinical, even salicious enquiry is necessitated, the society reports, by the 'paucity of materials' pertaining to New York's Dutch past and the 'extreme difficulty of procuring such as relate to [its] first settlement and colonial transactions'. It requested donations of 'Manuscripts, Records, Pamphlets and Books relative to the History of this Country', in the hopes that any documents in private hands might help to inform New Yorkers about their collective past. Without these documents, the group warned, 'history will be nothing more than a well-combined series of ingenious conjectures and amusing fables.' They did not know that their warning would become a literary challenge in the decades to come.

It had been five years since the New-York Historical Society had been founded by state governor DeWitt Clinton and a high-profile handful of Manhattan luminaries, with the promise to serve as the city's pre-eminent storehouse of information and scholarship about New York State. In that time, to the society's surprise and dismay, no history had been found. Together, the Revolutionary War, the British occupation and numerous citywide fires had made short work of church records, government documents and family papers. The ledgers of New Amsterdam were intact at Albany, to be sure, but no one could translate them: the Dutch speaker charged with the task in 1805 had taken his fee and disappeared. Other states were able to furnish similar historical societies with abundant resources (such as Massachusetts) or even to publish lengthy accounts of their states' founding and development (Virginia and Delaware). Despite the fact that post-war New York had become the nation's foremost destination for sophistication and spectacle, hailed by a contemporary British visitor as 'the first city in the United States for wealth, commerce, and population', its citizens knew little more about their founding history than Henry Hudson had, 200 years before.

The city complicated the Historical Society's project by its very nature: nineteenth-century New York was in perpetual flux. The population had tripled since the Revolutionary War, and in 1806 more than 75,000 people called New York home. For Manhattanites the city's contours did not yet reflect this rapid growth: the nucleus of 'New-York' seemed the same as it had when the British evacuated the island in 1783. The most fashionable neighbourhood radiated out from the Battery, Bowling Green and lower Broadway, a short walk from the venerable Tontine Coffee House, New York's unofficial stock exchange, and Trinity Church, still the most fashionable house of worship. A close-knit merchant elite (whose numbers included the members of the New-York Historical Society) presided over this microcosmic Manhattan while their poorer neighbours pushed the edges of the city northwards, nearer to the ancient ponds of New Amsterdam that had long since been polluted with runoff from nearby tanneries – particularly the Collect Pond, which had been drained and filled in 1811, but would soon begin to fill the neighbourhood around it, now known as Five Points, with toxic mud and a methane stench. The cornerstone of the first Roman Catholic cathedral in New York, to be called St Patrick's, had just been laid on

Five Points, print based on an earlier painting of 1827 by George Catlin.

THE LOCATION OF THE FIVE POINTS

'Debauchery has made the very houses old,' Charles Dickens wrote in *American Notes* after a visit to the Five Points, the red-light district of nineteenth-century New York. It is hard to find the Five Points today, except in historical novels and Scorsese films: not all of the streets that once made up its borders still exist. The original 'points' were Cross Street (now Mosco Street), Anthony Street (now Worth), Orange Street (now Baxter), Mulberry Street and Little Water Street (which has been replaced by the New York County Courthouse).

Five Points was hard by the Collect Pond, which had once been a source of fresh water for the New Amsterdam colony and was later a picnic destination and, most famously, the site of Robert Fulton's trial of a paddle-wheel steamship in 1796. By the early nineteenth century, however, it had become a toxic swamp, and was filled in by the city (it is now partly occupied by Foley Square park). The landfill did not exactly take: within a decade the neighbourhood began to stink — and the buildings to sink. Only those who could not afford to go elsewhere stayed in the Five Points, and it remained New York's epicentre of crime and disease for nearly a century before the photojournalism of Jacob A. Riis and others prompted the city to raze most of the tenements. Columbus Park, which sits on the southwestern edge of Chinatown, is the closest most visitors come to finding the Five Points, unless they have reason to visit one of the court-house or municipal buildings that surround Foley Square.

Mott Street, between Bowery and Broadway, but the location was so far north of the urban centre that it seemed like another country. Manhattan's new City Hall was also north of the residential district, at the top of the Old Commons: half a million dollars' worth of Berkshire marble carved into half a dozen competing architectural styles. The north side of this extravagant temple to democracy, facing Chambers Street, was not clad in marble but in cheaper brownstone, on the assumption that few citizens of quality would see the building from that vantage, so far 'uptown'.

It is hard to reconcile the humility of that decision with the ambition of New York's Common Council, which voted in 1807 to authorize the surveying of the entire island of Manhattan above Houston Street. The city was to be laid out in 'streets, roads, and public squares, of such width, extent, and direction, as to them shall seem most conducive to public good', the Council decreed, assigning the task of taming Manhattan's wilderness to a young engineer named John Randel Jr. The Randel Plan, an orderly grid of numbered streets and avenues, comprises the map of New York to this day. It was the work of a fortune-teller: Randel and his team of surveyors had to predict the march of business and residential neighbourhoods towards the top of Manhattan Island, and anticipate sprawl that would take almost a century to arrive. At the time of Randel's survey, actual sheep grazed on the future site of Sheep Meadow in Central Park, while farms, shantytowns and Seneca Village, a community of slaves freed by the Manumission Act of 1799, occupied the wooded northern reaches that would later be the Fifth Avenue stretch most favoured by Gilded Age tycoons. The Randel Plan organized these disparate properties into tidy blocks and lots: even Peter Stuyvesant's famous 'Bouwerie', now inhabited by the governor's descendants, was sliced into pieces by the inexorable progress of First, Second and Third Avenues towards the Harlem River. It was no wonder that the Historical Society worried that progress would destroy any remaining chances they had at recovering a true narrative of New York's past.

But when the first threat to the project of historical recovery arrived, it came in the form of a hoax: a mysterious book that appeared on 6 December 1809 (a day that was still observed by Dutch New Yorkers as St Nicholas's Day) with the unwieldy title of

> A History of New-York, from the Beginning of the World to the End of the Dutch Dynasty; Containing, among Many Surprising and Curious Matters, the Unutterable Ponderings of Walter the Doubter, the Disastrous Projects of William the Testy, and the Chivalric Achievements of Peter the Headstrong – The Three Dutch Governors of New Amsterdam: Being the Only Authentic History of the Times that Ever Hath Been or Ever Will Be Published.

The author of this nearly 300-page tome was given as 'Diedrich Knickerbocker', but the creator is better known to posterity as the author and humourist Washington Irving, whose only previous claim to fame was shared responsibility for coining the nickname 'Gotham' for the city of New York. The *History of New York* was a strange book, even by early nineteenth-century standards: it was a humorous, sometimes bawdy account of the discovery, colonization, cultivation and ultimate loss of the New Amsterdam settlement, as told from the perspective of Knickerbocker, a mouthy Dutch descendant of the original colonists. Knickerbocker insists that nearly all of New York's characteristic features must be credited to his ancestors: the twisty streets of lower Manhattan are the work of Dutch cows, and New Yorkers' fondness for doughnuts the work of Dutch *vrouws*. More importantly, he argues for New York's exceptionalism, and suggests that readers look to New Amsterdam for the historical consciousness that the city fathers claimed had been lost. Nearly 200 years before Saul Steinberg's famous cartoon, Knickerbocker, claiming Herodotus as his inspiration, situates Manhattan at the centre of the known universe, and the genre of the New York story was born.

Knickerbocker's *History* brought its author fame on both sides of the Atlantic – even Sir Walter Scott was a fan of the young American's satire. But Irving's work, however celebrated, was not the kind of history that the Historical Society had in mind

Washington Irving by John Wesley Jarvis, 1809.

when appealing to the public: it was, first and foremost, a work of fiction, one that (to the dismay of serious-minded citizens) gave rise to a legion of 'Knickerbocker' imitators, who slapped the name on any political view, commercial product or cultural output that had a New York flavour. The latter included the *Knickerbocker Magazine*, which would help to launch many of the first literary talents of independent New York, as well as to incubate a publishing industry that would grow, over the course of the century, into a juggernaut. A certain cosmopolitan decorum links most of these early New York writers, many of whom moved fluidly from fiction to journalism and back again. Their theme is, invariably, the quicksilver city growing up around them, or, as essayist Nathaniel Parker Willis put it, the daily 'fluxes and refluxes' of Broadway. One Knickerbocker poet famous in his day but forgotten to posterity was Fitz-Greene Halleck, whose celebrated mock epic 'Fanny' gently lampooned the pretensions of upwardly mobile Gothamites, including the fact that the prejudice against 'bridge and tunnel' destinations (such as Brooklyn and Staten Island) existed long before there were bridges or tunnels in the city:

> His travels had extended to Bath races;
> And Bloomingdale and Bergen he had seen,
> And Harlæm Heights; and many other places,
> By sea and land, had visited; and been,
> In a steamboat of the Vice President's,
> To Staten-Island once – for fifty cents.

In their own day, 'Knickerbocker' writers were charged with timidity and accused of aping their English cousins as a guarantee of commercial success. New York had recently suffered under the British trade embargo during the war of 1812, a fresh reminder that the liberties Americans enjoyed were still of tender age. Even Irving, despite his early audacity, came under fire for falling back on nostalgic, Anglo-Saxon themes in his post-Knickerbocker work. Philip Freneau, a proponent of American regional culture, called Irving to task in 'To a New England Poet' of 1823, a poem that urges (with some sarcasm) young American writers to go abroad for literary celebrity:

> Why stay in such a tasteless land,
> Where all must on a level stand,
> (Excepting people, at their ease,
> Who choose the level where they please:)
> See Irving gone to Britain's court
> To people of another sort,
> He will return, with wealth and fame,
> While Yankees hardly know your name.

Freneau's warning of a 'tasteless land' was echoed by another critic, the young Edgar Allan Poe, who had been sent to report on the 'Doings of Gotham' by the Pennsylvania newspaper the

Wall Street, looking west towards Trinity Church, 1847.

Columbian Spy. 'I could not look on the magnificent cliffs, and
stately trees, which at every moment met my view,' he says of
a Manhattan vista, 'without a sigh for their inevitable doom
– inevitable and swift. In twenty years, or thirty at farthest, we
shall see here nothing more romantic than shipping, warehouses,
and wharves.' Change was fast becoming the constant of
New York: in the decades between Irving's rhapsody and Poe's
prediction, the city had been scorched by yet another disastrous
fire and had suffered the first of several financial panics. Yellow
fever and cholera epidemics had left their own mark on the
urban landscape: Greenwich Village was developed at this time
by New Yorkers fleeing to healthier neighbourhoods. At the
same time, change meant progress: gas for public street lamps,
fresh water from the Croton Aqueduct and the beginnings of
a much-needed citywide sewer system, not to mention the
1825 opening of the Erie Canal, which connected the Atlantic
Ocean with the Great Lakes, and made New York's port the
most important in the country. Despite all this transformation,

a restive Poe remarked that 'the literary world of New York is not particularly busy.' Poe, who is rarely described as a New York writer, was in fact the beneficiary of this not-busy 'literary world': his poem 'The Raven' first appeared in the *New York Evening Mirror*, which led to the publication of collections of his stories and poems by the New York publisher Wiley & Putnam. Given this welcome, it is surprising that Poe chose to completely ignore the city in his work. Even his fictionalized account of the murder of Mary Rogers, a pretty Manhattan 'cigar girl' whose mangled body was discovered in the Hudson River in 1841, is set not in New York, but Paris.

Regardless of the change in venue, Poe's tabloid topic prefigured the next popular wave of fiction to emerge from New York: the gaslight genre. Gaslight books grew out of the success of English 'penny dreadfuls', inexpensive, serialized books on sensational or lurid themes. They shared the production values and aesthetic of their English counterparts, but focused on urban prurience and purported truth rather than romance. One of the high priests of American gaslight was George C. Foster, author of *New York in Slices, by an Experienced Carver* (1849) and *New York by Gaslight* (1850). His books promised to give readers 'true' glimpses of the 'very rotting skeleton of City Civilization', particularly the 'thick and putrid atmosphere' of the Five Points, with its population of 'rowdies negroes drunken sailors pickpockets burglars and vagabonds of every description'. Foster's exposés were inflated, bigoted and written in the purplest of prose, but the true story of New York at mid-century was hardly less dramatic than the gaslight version. The population of New York County more than tripled between 1800 and 1830, and by 1855, the New York State census would report that more than half of the city's residents were foreign-born. This boom strained New York's municipal resources, revealing, in the process, the prejudices of many of the city's self-proclaimed 'natives'. The Potato Famine of 1845 would bring more than half a million Irish to New York's shores, but even before this influx, the steady arrival of white European immigrants and of freed and runaway slaves had had an impact on living conditions in the poorer sections

Edgar Allan Poe,
1848.

of the city. As early as 1833, Five Points and other overcrowded
neighbourhoods had been the targets of several institutional
'slum clearance' campaigns led by the new Society for the
Prevention of Pauperism. These met with little success, and
by the time of the famine, New York's tenements were – as
Foster's works suggest – international tourist attractions. The
fact that so many of New York's poor were either immigrants
or African American only made their wealthier neighbours
more fascinated and fearful, and resulted in numerous wide-
scale riots between rival ethnicities and warring gangs. These
clashes primarily involved the poorest and the newest New
Yorkers, but they revealed religious and ethnic fissures that
affected everyone.

The writers Herman Melville and Walt Whitman may be
said to have emerged from this crucible of change. Certainly, the
city was now different from the one Melville's patrician Dutch
ancestors, the Gansevoorts, settled in. The writer himself was
born in New York Cityand raised there until the age of eleven,
when his family decamped for better economic prospects in

'Our Homeless Poor': early morning in Donovan Lane, near the Five Points.

Albany. He would not return to Manhattan until he was 28, and then for just three years. During his lifetime, he was most famous for his fictionalized accounts of sea voyages and exotic Polynesian soujourns, such as *Typee*, *Omoo*, *Redburn* and *White-jacket* – many of which he wrote during his return to New York. And yet the book that assures his lasting fame as a New York writer is the one that was all but ignored during his lifetime: *Moby-Dick*, which was published in 1851. Melville's now-celebrated story of the monomaniacal sea captain and

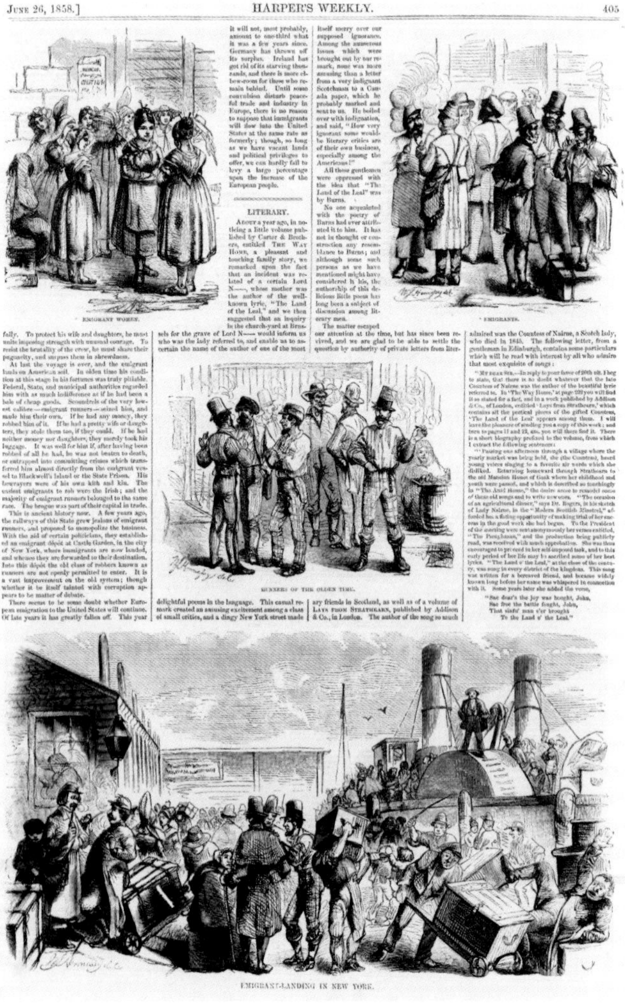

June 26, 1858.] HARPER'S WEEKLY. 405

EMIGRANT WOMEN.

EMIGRANTS.

fully. To protect his wife and daughters, he must unite imposing strength with unusual courage. To resist the brutality of the crew, he must share their pugnacity, and surpass them in shrewdness.

At last the voyage is over, and the emigrant lands on American soil. In olden time his condition at this stage in his fortunes was truly pitiable. Federal, State, and municipal authorities regarded him with as much indifference as if he had been a bale of cheap goods. Scoundrels of the very lowest calibre—emigrant runners—seized him, and made him their own. If he had any money, they robbed him of it. If he had a pretty wife or daughters, they stole them too, if they could. If he had neither money nor daughters, they merely took his luggage. It was well for him if, after having been robbed of all he had, he was not beaten to death, or entrapped into committing crimes which transferred him almost directly from the emigrant vessel to Blackwell's Island or the State Prison. His betrayers were of his own kith and kin. The easiest emigrants to rob were the Irish; and the majority of emigrant runners belonged to the same race. The brogue was part of their capital in trade.

This is ancient history now. A few years ago, the railways of this State grew jealous of emigrant runners, and proposed to monopolize the business. With the aid of certain politicians, they established an emigrant dépôt at Castle Garden, in the city of New York, where immigrants are now landed, and whence they are forwarded to their destination. Into this dépôt the old class of robbers known as runners are not openly permitted to enter. It is a vast improvement on the old system; though whether it be itself tainted with corruption appears to be matter of debate.

There seems to be some doubt whether European emigration to the United States will continue. Of late years it has greatly fallen off. This year it will not, most probably, amount to one-third what it was a few years since. Germany has thrown off its surplus. Ireland has got rid of its starving thousands, and there is more elbow-room for those who remain behind. Until some convulsion disturb peaceful trade and industry in Europe, there is no reason to suppose that immigrants will flow into the United States at the same rate as formerly; though, so long as we have vacant lands and political privileges to offer, we can hardly fail to levy a large percentage upon the increase of the European people.

LITERARY.

About a year ago, in noticing a little volume published by Carter & Brothers, entitled The Way Home, a pleasant and touching family story, we remarked upon the fact that an incident was related of a certain Lord N——, whose mother was the author of the well-known lyric, "The Land of the Leal," and we then suggested that an inquiry in the church-yard at Brussels for the grave of Lord N—— would inform us who was the lady referred to, and enable us to ascertain the name of the author of one of the most delightful poems in the language. This casual remark created an amusing excitement among a class of small critics, and a dingy New York street made itself merry over our supposed ignorance. Among the numerous issues which were brought out by our remark, none was more amusing than a letter from a very indignant Scotchman to a Canada paper, which he probably marked and sent to us. He boiled over with indignation, and said, "How very ignorant some would-be literary critics are of their own business, especially among the Americans!"

All these gentlemen were oppressed with the idea that "The Land of the Leal" was by Burns.

No one acquainted with the poetry of Burns had ever attributed it to him. It has not in thought or construction any resemblance to Burns; and although some such persons as we have mentioned might have considered it his, the authorship of this delicious little poem has long been a subject of discussion among literary men.

The matter escaped our attention at the time, but has since been revived, and we are glad to be able to settle the question by authority of private letters from literary friends in Scotland, as well as of a volume of Lays from Strathearn, published by Addison & Co., in London. The author of the song so much admired was the Countess of Nairne, a Scotch lady, who died in 1845. The following letter, from a gentleman in Edinburgh, contains some particulars which will be read with interest by all who admire that most exquisite of songs:

"My dear Sir,—In reply to your favor of 20th ult. I beg to state, that there is no doubt whatever that the late Countess of Nairne was the author of the beautiful lyric referred to. In 'The Way Home,' at page [illegible] you will find it so stated for a fact, and in a work published by Addison & Co., of London, entitled 'Lays from Strathearn,' which contains all the poetical pieces of the gifted Countess, 'The Land of the Leal' appears among them. I will have the pleasure of sending you a copy of this work; and turn to pages 11 and 12, etc., you will there find it. There is a short biography prefixed to the volume, from which I extract the following sentences:

"'Passing one afternoon through a village where the yearly market was being held, she (the Countess), heard young voices singing to a favorite air words which she disliked. Returning homeward through Strathearn to the old Mansion House of Gask where her childhood and youth were passed, and which is described so touchingly in "The Auld House," the desire arose to remodel some of these old songs and to write new ones. "The occasion of an agricultural dinner," says Dr. Rogers, in his sketch of Lady Nairne, in the "Modern Scottish Minstrel," afforded her a fitting opportunity of making trial of her success in the good work she had begun. To the President of the meeting were sent anonymously her verses entitled, "The Ploughman," and the production being publicly read, was received with much approbation. She was thus encouraged to proceed in her self-imposed task, and to this early period of her life may be ascribed some of her best lyrics. "The Land o' the Leal," at the close of the century, was sung in every district of the kingdom. This song was written for a bereaved friend, and became widely known long before her name was whispered in connection with it. Some years later she added the verse,

"Sae dear's the joy was bought, John,
Sae free the battle fought, John,
That sinfu' man e'er brought
To the Land o' the Leal."

RUNNERS OF THE OLDEN TIME.

EMIGRANT-LANDING IN NEW YORK.

W. J. Hennessy, four scenes of European immigrants in America, from *Harper's Weekly*, 28 June 1858.

Photograph of Walt
Whitman by George
C. Cox, 1887.

the white whale is set mostly at sea (after a brief stop in New
England), but it begins in the 'insular city of the Manhattoes',
a city which, according to Melville's narrator Ishmael, drives
men to her shorelines to stand 'fixed in ocean reveries', as 'nigh
the water as they can possibly get without falling in'. Ishmael's
invocation has never ceased to function as a siren song for
those who are enamoured with the island nature of New York,
and who find in the act of walking to its extremities – as well
as leaving from and returning to them – a transcendental joy.
This was the experience of the poet Walt Whitman, whose
'Crossing Brooklyn Ferry', from the collection *Leaves of Grass*,
hails New Yorkers as 'a generation, or ever so many generations
hence', who share the same littoral vista as Whitman on the
ferry in 1856:

> The glories strung like beads on my smallest sights and
>   hearings – on the walk in the street, and the passage
>   over the river,
> The current rushing so swiftly, and swimming with me far
>   away . . .

Bird's-eye view of Manhattan, looking south from Union Square, *c.* 1849.

Whitman, a Long Island native, lived in Manhattan and Brooklyn until the Civil War and worked as a journalist, hack writer, politician, carpenter and all-around *flâneur*. His biographical collection, *Specimen Days*, sums up the transcendental ambitions that inform all his work: 'what I may call the human interior and exterior of these great seething oceanic populations . . . is to me best of all.' The same purpose informs his poetry collection *Leaves of Grass*, which received mixed reviews in the poet's lifetime (Emerson wrote Whitman a letter of guarded praise, while Rufus Griswold deemed the book 'a gathering of muck [and] . . . gross obscenity'), but is now recognized as the closest thing we have to an audio recording of nineteenth-century New York. Whitman catches at the sounds of the city at mid-century and encourages the reader to step out of the crowd – not only to look, but to listen:

> I think I will do nothing for a long time but listen,
> And accrue what I hear into myself . . . and let sounds
>   contribute toward me.
> . . .
> I hear the sound of the human voice . . . a sound I love,
> I hear all sounds as they are tuned to their uses . . .
>   sounds of the city and sounds out of the city . . .
>   sounds of the day and night;
> . . .
> . . . this indeed is music![4]

Whitman, sounding his 'barbaric yawp over the roofs of the world', ushered New Yorkers into an exhilarating and explosive new world.

In July 1861 a writer named T. Addison Richards 'circum-navigated' New York for *Harper's New Monthly Magazine*, waxing rhapsodic about the pastoral reaches of Washington Heights and Harlem:

> The upper portion of our island yet presents, – upon the Hudson side as upon the East, very much of its primitive forest look; and for more than half the distance of the fourteen miles between the Spuyten Duyvl and the Battery, the shore is as yet but little disturbed by the city encroachments, excepting [the occasional] factory dock, an embryo street, or . . . village nucleus.

The southern tip of this 'far-famed island city' presented a very different aspect, however: instead of 'mossy hillocks' a circum-navigator would have seen thousands of soldiers camped out in the Battery and City Hall Parks, and homes and storefronts draped in patriotic bunting from the foot of Broadway up to Union Square. The Civil War had begun at Fort Sumter in South Carolina that April, and Manhattan had once again been chosen as the headquarters of the United States Army. Facing this new reality, New Yorkers set aside their political differences and closed ranks – at least for the time being. The Civil War was never fought on New York soil, and yet it trans-formed the city in previously unimaginable ways. It gave a voice to immigrants, particularly Irish immigrants, and to African Americans. It unleashed the full power of private capital on the United States government. It galvanized the creation of major municipal and cultural institutions. And

Panoramic view of the waterfront of New York city (centre), Brooklyn (right), Jersey City (left) and the quarantine station on Staten Island (foreground), c. 1850.

it created the conditions necessary for an entirely new class of New Yorker: the professional social climber.

The city's flag-draped streets cloaked a very recent and deep ambivalence about the necessity of war with the South. A month before shots were fired on Fort Sumter, many prominent New Yorkers had hastily organized an 'American Society for Promoting National Unity' in the hopes of reaching a last-ditch compromise with the states threatening secession. As soon as war was declared, however, those same individuals threw their energies and their funds into the creation of civilian organizations with the influence and resources to make a deep impact on the lives of those affected by the war. Chief among these was the United States Sanitary Commission, a committee authorized by the federal government to provide medical, sanitary and financial assistance to volunteer Union soldiers during and after the war. Guided in part by Frederick Law Olmsted, the architect of Central Park, the Commission proved to be an invaluable resource, noteworthy for its efficient organization and skill at marshalling human capital. Among this human capital were

the social leaders of New York, well-born women who threw themselves into volunteer work for the Commission and organized massive fundraisers, dubbed 'Metropolitan Fairs', for its support. These fairs were held everywhere from Chicago to Philadelphia, but the Manhattan fair – which featured a 'Knickerbocker Kitchen' restaurant staffed by society ladies of Dutch descent – raised the most money. Another group based in New York was the Union Defense Committee, whose members included John Jacob Astor Jr and A. T. Stewart, the department store magnate. This committee took it upon themselves to manage and disburse a million-dollar mayoral appropriation for the outfitting and maintenance of New York regiments. To those who might question the aptitude of private citizens for an assignment more typically given to elected officials, the Committee's response was this, in an official memo:

> It will not however be deemed arrogant if the Committee
> state that mainly owing to the exertions of city and citizens
> of New York . . . an army has been placed in the field
> armed and equipped for the defense of the national cause
> in a shorter space of time and with less expenditure of

money than so far as any record shows has ever before been accomplished by any government.

Still other powerful people, such as the millionaire financier August Belmont, went abroad to persuade the British and French not to continue their trade with the Confederacy. New Yorkers were taking charge.

But not all of New York's citizens threw themselves into the war effort with a convert's fervour. In July 1863 a four-day draft riot overran the city from City Hall to Central Park. The riot began the day after the federal government began enforced conscription into the Union Army, with a provision for paid military substitutes (the princely sum of $300). Few working-class New Yorkers could afford a substitute, and few residents of tenement wards such as the Five Points saw any patriotic reason to give their livelihoods (and possibly lives) for the Union cause, particularly the cause of slave emancipation. The rage of these potential conscripts was brutally vented on African Americans: as many as 50 black New Yorkers were lynched during the rioting, and the city's Colored Orphan Asylum was burned to the ground (after its 233 children were escorted to safety). Black-owned businesses were destroyed and thousands of African Americans were driven from their homes. The residences and businesses of wealthy white New York merchants, politicians and abolitionists were also targeted, from Gramercy Square to Brooks Brothers Clothiers (tailors to New York's well-heeled Seventh Regiment). Railroads were torn up, the *New York Tribune* building was attacked and the mayor's residence and some police stations burned. Troops of soldiers were recalled from the battlefield to quell the violence, but the riots only finally ended when the u.s. Army temporarily suspended the draft. The monumental influence of the Empire City could not have been made more apparent: not war, but the collective action of several thousand angry New Yorkers had brought the federal government to a grinding halt.

The draft resumed peacefully, but the city retained its political authority throughout the war and the reconstruction that followed. Many New York manufacturers profited from the supply of munitions to the Union Army, and the development of a national banking system and a uniform national currency after Reconstruction enabled many of the city's financiers to become (as groups like the Union Defense Committee had intimated) the creditors of the federal government. At the same time, the patronage politics of state senator 'Boss' William Magear Tweed, ascendant at Tammany Hall, made sure that New York's government never lacked cronies or creditors of its

Cartoon by Thomas Nast that reflects the sham formality of 'Boss' Tweed's arrest (he was immediately released on bail). Lady Justice, behind the arresting officers, is not amused.

own. These two kinds of 'bosses' moved in very different circles, but it is nevertheless a challenge to untangle their impact on the physical and cultural development of New York City. Tweed, who collected political appointments, directorships and bribes like so many raindrops, was possibly the most corrupt politician the city has endured to date. His name is now a metonym for graft, but he also displayed a quintessential New York chutzpah: he ran Tammany for twenty years before he was charged with embezzlement, and even then he had to be arrested three times (on one occasion he was released and re-elected, and on another he fled to Spain). At the height of his influence, he pushed the development of fashionable neighbourhoods such as the Upper East and West sides and obtained a prime plot of land for the Metropolitan Museum of Art. The emerging captains of industry and business were also transforming real estate in Manhattan.

The 'Petit Chateau', William K. Vanderbilt's residence in New York.

A view of A. T. Stewart's 'Marble Palace' department store on lower Fifth Avenue.

They may never have spent $12 million on a courthouse, as Tweed did in the over twenty years it took to build the Old New York County Courthouse (now Tweed Courthouse), but William K. Vanderbilt easily spent $3 million on his 'Petit Chateau', a French Renaissance confectioon the corner of Fifth and 52nd Street. A. T. Stewart's flagship store, the 'Marble Palace', was as big as any tycoon's chateau: it spanned the blocks between Broadway and Fourth Avenue, and between Ninth and Tenth Streets, much as Macy's department store spans the distance between Sixth and Seventh Avenues in Midtown Manhattan today. Stewart's store, staffed by 350 clerks, helped to transform Broadway into the city's 'nerve center for shopping and display'. It also helped to push the residential centre east, to Fifth Avenue, as *Leslie's Weekly* forecast with some prescience in 1865:

> Within the past few years, at certain times of the day . . . the Fifth avenue rivals Broadway seriously as a promenade. We have no doubt that the time will come, within a quarter of a

century, when fashion will change from Broadway to Fifth avenue entirely . . . and that the now fashionable avenue will be nothing but a row of stores for retail, while in Broadway the wholesale trade will have monopolized everything below 14th street.

The grand 'Breede Weg', fashionable nerve centre of New York for centuries, was about to be replaced.

Hand in hand with 'fashion', culture moved north and east through the city. Central Park had created a cosmopolitan vista for real-estate pioneers like the Vanderbilts, who could now build their mansions on the quiet upper stretches of Fifth Avenue, secure in the knowledge that their address was no longer beyond society's pale. By 1877 the American Museum of Natural History (which had begun in the Central Park Arsenal in 1869) anchored the west side of Central Park, and in 1880 the Metropolitan Museum (founded in 1872) would open its Calvert Vaux and Jacob Wrey Mould-designed Gothic building on the east side. The venerable Academy of Music at Union Square had been supplanted by the Metropolitan Opera, which opened at Broadway and 39th in 1883 with the support of John Jacob Astor II, J. P. Morgan, William Rockefeller and assorted Vanderbilts who had been shut out of the old-money Academy. The increasingly evident wealth, philanthropy and arts patronage of families such as these does not seem to have been markedly diminished by the Panic of 1873 or the six years of depression that followed it; rather, it was New York's bankers who helped President Ulysses S. Grant re-establish national credit in the wake of it. In the meantime, the 'Upper Ten Thousand' continued to grow, and with it an efflorescence of artisanal cottage industries, including everything from the exquisite carvings of sculptor Augustus Saint-Gaudens and blazing stained glass of John LaFarge and Louis Comfort Tiffany, to the Beaux-Arts architecture of Richard Morris Hunt (creator of the 'Petit Chateau') and the firm of McKim, Mead & White. Inevitably these publicly private displays of wealth and grandeur gave rise to yet another cottage industry: that of the society celebrity.

The 'Angel of the Waters' statue at Bethesda Fountain in Central Park is the work of Emma Stebbins, the first woman to receive a public art commission in New York City.

'I believe in a republic,' Mrs William Astor told *The Delineator* in 1908, 'and I believe in a republic in which money has a great deal to say, as in ours. Money represents with us energy and character; it is acquired by brains and untiring effort; it is kept intact only by the same means.' Money like Mrs Astor's not only talked – it was universally persuasive. It made media darlings out of the wives of magnates and had, by the beginning of the twentieth century, transformed dozens of American debutantes into European princesses. Mrs Astor, the descendant of patrician Dutch settlers and a shipping heiress, is often credited with jump-starting the Gilded Age at her first 'Four Hundred' ball, held in February 1892. The 'Four Hundred' was meant to be a figure of precision, a number based on the capacity of Mrs Astor's (admittedly cavernous) Fifth Avenue ballroom, but the list, when shared with the *New York Times*, turned out to contain the names of only 263 guests. Perhaps because the 'Four Hundred' proved to be even more

INVENTING THE SOCIAL REGISTER

The *Social Register* was not the first catalogue of wealthy and well-born citizens of nineteenth-century New York. That distinction may go to a *New York Sun* pamphlet of 1845 entitled *Wealth and Biography of the Wealthy Citizens of New York City: comprising an alphabetical arrangement of persons estimated to be worth $100,000 and upwards*. This little document, compiled by Moses Yale Beach, the founder of the Associated Press, was no *Debrett's Peerage*: it mixed 'Knickerbocker' Dutch families with affluent New Yorkers of English descent, as well as with recent immigrants such as the German-born fur trader John Jacob Astor, whose fortune the *Sun* underestimated at $10 million. The *Social Register*, which first appeared 42 years later, did aspire to be an American *Debrett's*, and since 1887, it has compiled and published an 'accurate and careful list' of 'society', as defined by the anonymous and secretive editors of the Social Register Association, its New York-based publisher.

The first edition of the *Register* included sections on 'departures and foreign addresses', 'engaged', 'married', 'deaths' and 'club elections' (the Century, Knickerbocker, Union and Tuxedo Club were among those the *Register* deemed 'leading clubs'), and the sections have changed little over the years since then. No definition of American 'society' has ever been offered by the Social Register Association; nor, lacking a bona fide aristocracy, has it ever suggested by what science or art it arrives at its 'accurate and careful' list of American socialites. Perhaps this is why the *Register* endures: it derives its lasting influence from its ineffability. It also, however, derives its influence from its ability to (quietly, tacitly) absorb the nouveau riche: John Jacob Astor's namesake grandson is not only catalogued in the *Register*'s first edition, but listed as a 'patron' of the book itself.

Brooklyn-born Mrs John Jacob Astor IV (Madeleine Talmadge Force) survived the sinking of the Titanic, in which her husband died.

Looking southeast from behind the Statue of Liberty, 1978.

exclusive than the name promised, the epithet, and the idea of a 'master' list for New York society, appealed to the imaginations – and imaginative snobbery – of New Yorkers rich and poor. That did not keep them from contesting the validity of her Olympus-like pronouncements, however. 'I am an unbeliever in the body corporate which, for want of a better term, has come to be popularly known as the Four Hundred of New York', a Mrs Burton Harrison wrote in *The Cosmopolitan* in 1895. 'The lists of visits and invitations made out yearly by people of good position, to include their acquaintances to whom such courtesies are due, number, say, a thousand names. Of these names, who among us is equipped or prepared to say six hundred are outside the pale?' Many people, as it turned out, felt themselves equipped to make this judgement, including the editors of New York's first society tabloid, *Town Topics*. The magazine covered the news and gossip created by (and for) people of fashion up and down the Eastern seaboard, as well as in Chicago, and specialized in lists of private balls (the better to know where you weren't invited) and scandalous, barely blind items, including one that reportedly ended the marriage of the most famous American arbiter of manners, Emily Post.

The new, ever more extravagant manifestations of wealth and exclusivity that preoccupied the upper echelons of New York society were diagnosed by the sociologist Thorstein Veblen in his 1899 text *The Theory of the Leisure Class*. 'Conspicuous consumption', he argued, was the last occupation of the purposefully idle – the leisure class. By 1892, 27 per cent of all American millionaires lived in New York City. Lacking all else to do, it behooved them (or their wives and families) to commission the creation of beautiful objects; found and join private clubs (New York had more than twenty gentlemen's clubs by 1900) and restrictive genealogical societies (such as the Colonial Order of the Acorn, which required members to be direct patrilineal descendants of the pre-Revolutionary colonies); endow major charities; and host decadent dinners where guests were greeted by live swans swimming in a lake in the centre of the dining table. It was a world that Henry James had touched on in his major novels (particularly in his New

York real-estate ghost story, 'The Jolly Corner'), but the true
bard of the Four Hundred, Edith Wharton, was only just
beginning to chronicle the caste into which she had been born.
By 1905, when Wharton's *House of Mirth* was published, the
tribes of Fifth Avenue were well into their second generation.
What fuelled this frantic enumeration of the gilded ranks, the
endless need to calibrate the 'in' and 'out' crowds? One answer
lies in New York Harbor: the Ellis Island Immigration Bureau,
which opened in 1892 to the *New York Times* headline, 'Landed
on Ellis Island – New Immigration Buildings Opened Yesterday.
Rosy-cheeked Irish Girl the First Registered'. Charming teenager 'Annie Moore . . . lately a resident of County Cork and
yesterday one of the 148 steerage passengers landed from the
Guion ship Nevada' may not have noticed, as she was registered
with some fanfare and presented with a $10 coin, but she was a
stand-in for the zeitgeist. By 1900 a full one-third of New York's
nearly 3.5 million residents were foreign-born.

By the end of the nineteenth century, New York City
had assembled a fairly complete portrait of itself. Through
guidebooks, memoirs and novels, wealthy New Yorkers in
particular had learned how to reminisce convincingly about a
past they may not have shared. They commissioned family trees,

Immigrants arriving at Ellis Island.

An owl's-eye view of Herald Square, 1899, showing the 6th Avenue elevated train, Broadway and the Tabernacle, and the defunct *New York Herald* newspaper building in the centre; print by Charles William Jefferys.

designed ancestral crests and preserved historic homesteads, the better to prove their authentic connection to Washington Irving's 'real lords of the soil'. In the never-ending effort to get in (and stay in) Manhattan's 'Knickerbocracy', they had become increasingly philanthropic and civic-minded and had memorized the names on the city's social roster, even as that exalted pantheon continued to shift. But none of this would count as preparation for the kinetic upheavals of the century to come, which would render the city unrecognizable to itself in the best and worst of ways.

'Father Knickerbocker's Last Day as a Bachelor', the *New York Times* headline announced on 1 January 1898. Manhattan was getting married, in a matter of speaking: the consolidation of Manhattan, Brooklyn (then second only to Manhattan in population), Queens, Staten Island and the Bronx into the single city known as 'Greater New York' was about to be made official. New York, already the largest city in the United States, had just left the competition in the dust. 'The Imperial city has won an honorable renown throughout the world,' declared parks commissioner Andrew Haswell Green, the dogged architect of consolidation, '[one] which all her colonies may proudly inherit

Father Knickerbocker proposing consolidation to Miss Brooklyn; the East River stands between them, and the newly constructed Brooklyn Bridge is in the distance. *Puck*, 18 January 1893.

The wedge-shaped Flatiron Building at Fifth Avenue and 23rd Street, completed in 1902, is made of steel clad in limestone and glazed terracotta.

Interior view of Grand Central Terminal, which opened in 1913.

and which they cannot avoid accepting.' New York's 'imperial' destiny was indeed unavoidable at the turn of the new century, and it was writ large in the exuberant transformation of the city into something brand-new and sometimes quite strange – as strange as the vision of Charles Lindbergh taking off for Paris in 1927 from Roosevelt Field, or of Harry Houdini escaping in chains from a box submerged in the East River in 1912. The convergence of money and modernity in early twentieth-century New York was – quite literally – an electrifying phenomenon, and it left no corner of the city untouched.

Everything and everyone seemed to be happening in New York. The motion picture industry (which was launched at Koster and Bial's Music Hall at Broadway and 34th in 1896), the Ziegfeld Follies, birth control and the Steamship *Slocum* disaster. It didn't matter what it was – it was in New York first. Some of these transformations were all but invisible to the passer-by, such as the New York subway system, late to the rapid-transit movement but fully twice as large as its closest rival, the London Underground. Others were impossible to miss, such as the steel-framed skyscrapers that now scribbled on the skyline with a seemingly indelible optimism. The photographer Alfred Stieglitz often took the 21-storey Flatiron building (1902) as his subject, describing it as being like 'the bow of a monster ocean steamer – a picture of new America still in the making'. It was arguably New York in the making, too: propulsively moving forward, with little thought for all that had been left behind with Father Knickerbocker and the nineteenth century.

Money and modernity conspired together to benefit New Yorkers in innumerable ways in the early 1900s. Two palatial

The Plaza Hotel and Central Park, *c.* 1905.

A year after the *General Slocum* disaster, the cover of *Puck* magazine shows a weeping statue of Justice, with the burning ship sinking in the distance.

THE *GENERAL SLOCUM* DISASTER

Prior to 9/11, the burning and sinking of the *General Slocum* excursion steamboat was the disaster with the most fatalities in the history of New York City. The *General Slocum* set out on the morning of 15 June 1904 to take the congregation of St Mark's German Lutheran Church to a picnic outing on the shore of Long Island. On the wooden vessel were 1,331 passengers, most of them women and children from the Lower East Side German community known as Kleindeutschland, Little Germany – and few of them could swim. The fire was discovered shortly after the coal-fired steamboat set off up the East River, but the ship's fire hoses and life jackets proved to be rotten and useless, and the captain, his boat stuck among the rocks of Hell Gate, could not steer to shore in time to evacuate his passengers or prevent total immolation.

At least 1,021 people died in the fire, and the tragedy is often given as the reason for the migration of New York's German community north to Yorkville. The owners of the *General Slocum* were indicted, but only the captain was convicted of neglect of duty and sent to prison at Sing Sing, while the charred boat was sold and converted into a barge dubbed the *Maryland*, which sank off the coast of New Jersey in 1911. The last survivor of the *General Slocum* disaster died in 2004 at the age of 100: she had been six months old at the time of the fire.

railway stations punctuated Midtown: Grand Central Terminal, at Lexington and 42nd Street, which housed the trains of the New York Central Railroad; and the McKim, Mead & White-designed Pennsylvania Station near the Hudson River, which accommodated the Pennsylvania line. Hotels grew like their skyscraper cousins: Gilded Age palaces such as the Astor-owned Knickerbocker Hotel now kept company with tall and glamorous rivals such as the St Regis, the Roosevelt and the Biltmore, the last resembling a Richard Morris Hunt chateau on stilts. Hotels such as these (along with restaurants such as the 21 Club) replaced the tight-lipped set of the 'Four Hundred' with a publicity-hungry 'café society' whose exuberance was barely dampened by the ratification of Prohibition in 1919. Jazz Age chronicler F. Scott Fitzgerald even used the Biltmore as a kind of shorthand for the delirium of modernity in 'May Day' (1920), a story that features two drunken party guests who ride an elevator to the hotel's top floor, only to decide it's not high enough. 'Have another floor put on,' they tell the elevator operator. Given the speed of the city's technological progress, the request has a certain giddy logic. More giddy logic could be found outside the city limits, at Coney Island,

An aerial image of Grand Central Terminal. The elevated section of Park Avenue is visible: this innovation allowed the trains to enter the terminal from underground, rather than plough down the middle of a busy street, as they had previously done.

Night in Luna Park, Coney Island, 1905.

which had gone from seedy beach town to pre-eminent seaside attraction in a few short years, thanks to three enormous amusement parks: Steeplechase, Luna Park and Dreamland. All three exploited New York's fascination with the intersection of high and low culture: by day, they showcased engineering feats such as the Ferris wheel, the submarine, the nickelodeon and the airship, and by night they glittered with incandescent bulbs and suggestive, cinematic opportunities. Where else could a New Yorker go to try a hot dog (made famous in 1916 by restaurateur Nathan Handwerker), gawk at 'Bontoc Head Hunters' imported from the recently annexed Philippines, watch a film by Thomas Edison and admire incubator babies sleeping in their newfangled bassinets? On a single summer day in 1906, over 200,000 postcards were sent from Coney Island: it was truly the 'people's playground'.

The people of New York were transforming, too: by 1910, almost 35 per cent of New York City's residents were foreign-born, with the greatest numbers arriving from Eastern Europe and southern Italy, to join their predominantly Irish forerunners in neighbourhoods throughout the city. This

Pushcart shopping on Mulberry Street, once an enclave for Italian immigrant families, c. 1900.

explosion of new immigrants was a source of no small concern for New Yorkers, who were as fascinated and horrified by their new neighbours as ever. The potent mixture of curiosity and distaste was compounded by the fact that the most famous of the growing ethnic enclaves – Little Italy (also known as 'Mulberry Bend'), Chinatown and the Lower East Side – were either contained within or adjacent to the borders of the famously lawless Five Points area. The pre-existing prejudices of the xenophobic were only compounded by the First World War, which rendered any citizen with a 'homeland' allegiance (such as to Germany) an immediate threat. Speaking to the Knights of Columbus (a Catholic fraternal organization) in 1915, former president Theodore Roosevelt invoked the fears of many native-born Americans when he called new immigrants 'hyphenated Americans' and warned that citizens must be 'heartily and singly loyal to this Republic' or else be 'unsparingly condemn[ed]'. Five years later Lothrop Stoddard would publish *The Rising Tide of Color against White World-Supremacy*, a eugenics primer that would be parodied as 'The Rise of the Colored Empires' in F. Scott Fitzgerald's novel of 1925, *The*

Great Gatsby. 'The idea', Tom Buchanan harangues Nick Carraway, 'is if we don't look out the white race will be – will be utterly submerged. It's all scientific stuff; it's been proved.' Despite the intensity of Anglo-Saxon fist-shaking, new immigrants continued to be absorbed into the city, particularly in lower Manhattan and in East Harlem. These neighbourhoods became cultural havens for those fleeing persecution or penury, and places where the sounds and smells of home could be recreated and the native tongue spoken with impunity. They were also dangerously crowded: Kenneth Jackson reports that the average density of the Lower East Side in 1900 was 250,000 per square mile. Most of these new New Yorkers lived in 'dumbbell tenements', six-storey firetraps most famous for their warrens of tiny rooms and narrow, airless central courtyards. The plight of the tenement dweller was the subject of the photographer and writer Jacob Riis, whose poignant if prejudiced book *How the Other Half Lives* shone a bright light on the conditions of poor and newly arrived New Yorkers and ultimately inspired citywide tenement reform. Among Riis's contemporaries who took a hard look at

Street Arabs in Sleeping Quarters by Jacob Riis, c. 1880s.

Portrait of Langston Hughes by Carl Van Vechten, 1936.

the condition of the poor were the muckraking journalist Lincoln Steffens, whose 'Shame of the Cities' series placed the blame for working-class misery squarely on the shoulders of corrupt 'machine rule' and lobbied for 'government for the people', and Ida Tarbell, famous for her exposé of John D. Rockefeller's mammoth Standard Oil Corporation. Steffens, Riis and Tarbell were no genteel Junior Leaguers, but borrowed the tactics of the tabloids to expose injustice wherever they could. White working-class New Yorkers took up their own cause by mobilizing into trade unions, the better to bargain for improved wages and conditions, although many unions at the time also used their power to exclude African American workers. One notable early union was the International Ladies' Garment Workers' Union, founded in 1900 and famously galvanized by the Triangle Shirtwaist Fire of 1911, in which 146 female seamstresses died in a matter of minutes, trapped in their locked factory high above Washington Square Park.

African Americans were also carving out their place in Manhattan space and time as never before. The turn of the new century brought African Americans to New York in great numbers, including many who had left the post-war South in search of peace and opportunity. Painters, writers and cultural critics flocked to New York, seeking access to its increasingly famous (if hardly colour-blind) arts and publishing industries, its electric nightlife and the city's reputation as a crucible for ideas and innovation. Harlem, which had previously been a German Jewish neighbourhood, became 'The Mecca of the New Negro', in the words of the philosopher Alain Locke – the headquarters for all of these artistic communities. The creative

Duke Ellington directs his band during a radio broadcast, 1943.

capital of Harlem in the 1920s and '30s has few rivals in American history: the Harlem Renaissance nourished reform groups such as the National Association for the Advancement of Colored Peoples and the National League on Urban Conditions Among Negroes (now known as the National Urban League); supported black newspapers such as the *Amsterdam News*; nurtured literary magazines such as *The Crisis* and *Fire!*; and organized arts foundations, literary salons and nightclubs. Many seized upon Locke's exhortation to stop 'speaking for the Negro' and to begin to 'speak as Negroes' and threw themselves, as the painter Aaron Douglas did, into works celebrating African art and culture, or chose to reveal the hypocrisy of the colour line with meditations on blackness and the act of 'passing', as did the novelists Wallace Thurman and Nella Larsen. Beyond Harlem, however, New York struggled to catch up. In 'Dinner Guest: Me', Langston Hughes describes how 'demurely' and abstractly white New Yorkers treated 'The Negro Problem . . . The why and wherewithal / Of darkness USA – ', even as they 'wined and dined' him as a literary celebrity and dinner-party trophy. Patronizing the arts in Harlem was one thing, but a frank discussion of civil rights was another matter entirely. 'Solutions to the Problem, / Of course, wait', the poet concluded. The Problem did continue to 'wait' for decades, but the arrival in 1924 of both Louis Armstrong and Duke Ellington in New York opened up another avenue for the self-expression of Harlem, one that would catch the American imagination after the repeal of Prohibition in the 1930s and the beginning of the Swing Era – the birth of New York jazz.

A writer in early twentieth-century New York who was not in Harlem seemed to be one of two places: the Algonquin Hotel, in Midtown, or the White Horse Tavern, in Greenwich Village. This is, of course, a gross generalization, but the clusters of literary genius are hard to ignore. The Algonquin, on West 44th Street, was the home of the 'Round Table', a daily lunch club comprised of acid humourists and playwrights including Dorothy Parker, George S. Kaufman and Harold Ross, the editor of the *New Yorker* magazine, which had just begun publication in 1925. Downtown in the Village, the cobbled streets of Patchin Place and Cherry Lane were home to an assortment of original Bohemians, including the poets E. E. Cummings and Edna St Vincent Millay, the naturalist writer Theodore Dreiser and the novelist Djuna Barnes. The subject of New York insinuated itself into all their writings, as it had those of their literary forebears. Naturally, there were writers who did not inhabit either camp, such as Edith Wharton and F. Scott Fitzgerald. Both were haunted by the city from a distance and wrote their accounts of Manhattan 'tribes' (as Wharton called her Ur-Gilded Age clans) while living, for the most part, far from its electric din. The contemporary writer John Dos Passos, who lived in Brooklyn (as did the poet Hart Crane), does not have the same celebrity today, but his descriptions of New York capture the island's floodlit new strangeness and make him the modernist answer to Walt Whitman:

> Dusk gently smooths crispangled streets. Dark presses tight the steaming asphalt city, crushes the fretwork of windows and lettered signs and chimneys and watertanks and ventilators and fire-escapes and moldings and patterns and corrugations and eyes and hands and neckties into blue chunks, into black enormous blocks. Under the rolling heavier heavier pressure windows blurt light. Night crushes bright milk out of arclights, squeezes the sullen blocks until they drip red, yellow, green into streets resounding with feet. All the asphalt oozes light. Light spurts from lettering on roofs, mills dizzily among wheels, stains rolling tons of sky.

The 'heavier pressure' of New York had only just begun.

The Empire State Building, 1931.

In 1939, Parks Commissioner Robert Moses addressed the people of New York City in the pages of the *New York Times*. It was just two months before the grand opening of New York's World's Fair in Flushing Meadows, Queens, an extravaganza that heralded the future with the motto 'Building the World of Tomorrow'. This was a particularly cheering message for New Yorkers, who had seen the ebullience of the Jazz Age extinguished by the stock market crash of 1929 and the Great Depression that followed it. The Empire State Building, completed in 1931 on the site of President Franklin D. Roosevelt's ancestral family farm, was quickly dubbed the 'Empty State Building' for its lack of tenants, while 'Hoovervilles' (named after FDR's successor, Herbert Hoover), shanty towns for those left homeless by the Depression, sprang up in Central and Riverside Parks. Add to these discouragements the news that Europe stood on the brink of world war, and it must have seemed to New Yorkers that tomorrow could not come fast enough. But Moses wasn't interested in providing a sneak peek at the fair's attractions: he wanted to address the actual future of New York City – who would live there, and how. Moses had already been extremely effective at attracting federal funding to the city through Roosevelt's New Deal programme, the Works Progress Administration: by one estimate, $1 out of every $7 of the more than $13 billion appropriated for the WPA went to projects in New York City. Moses's vision was already being realized, as he points out in his editorial: by the time of the fair the commissioner had already instituted a 'comprehensive system of parks and parkways' to provide 'relief from strain

Mayor Fiorello LaGuardia in a train operator's cap, celebrating the opening of the 6th Avenue subway line, *c.* 1940.

and disorder' throughout Greater New York. Whether or not Moses's interborough system did in fact 'relieve' the city is still open for debate, but it is certainly evidence of Moses's unelected authority in the administration of Mayor Fiorello LaGuardia, and of his singleness of purpose. And that purpose, he insisted to New Yorkers awaiting the fair, was to make sure that the 'World of Tomorrow' was not unnavigable for the citydwellers of today. 'A Rip Van Winkle returning to New York City twenty or fifty years hence would be astonished at the changes,' he concluded, 'but he wouldn't be lost.'

The World's Fair itself, however, told a very different story. Instead of reflecting New York to the world, it reflected the world to New York – through the eyes of corporate executives, Hollywood producers and politicians. Even 'Democracity', a utopian model of a metropolis contained inside the Perisphere, a 180-foot in diameter hollow sphere that was one of the symbols of the fair (together with a spire called the Trylon), was quickly eclipsed by General Motors' Futurama, the largest scale model of a city constructed to date. The Futurama, which was the brainchild of the theatrical and industrial designer Norman Bel Geddes, took visitors through the city via 'carry-go-round' cars, which gave the same perspective as a bird or low-flying plane. It was by all accounts mesmerizing, and fairgoers stumbled out into the Queens sunshine proudly sporting 'I HAVE SEEN THE FUTURE' buttons and convinced of the need, as GM's press materials exhorted, for 'true highways to horizons of better living': in other words, the need for an interstate highway system – hardly an endorsement of dense city living. One of the most popular rides, the Eiffel-like Parachute Jump, was designed to train paratroopers in wartime and had been retrofitted with shock absorbers and a family-friendly corporate sponsor: Lifesavers. Still other exhibits capitalized on the national profile of the fair to bring the new motion picture celebrities to New York, including Marlene Dietrich, Dorothy Lamour, Douglas Fairbanks Jr, Johnny Weissmuller, Gene Autry and Donald Duck (who received an honorary degree from the fair), for photo ops that suggested that the future would in fact belong to the talent agencies. Tallulah Bankhead, star of Lillian Hellman's *The Little Foxes* on Broadway, opened the Ford Pavilion with a smile for the paparazzi, Babe Ruth signed baseballs, Benny Goodman jammed and even First Lady Eleanor Roosevelt gamely sported a Perisphere-and-Trylon-printed dress to launch the Finnish Relief Fund at the Finland Pavilion (Finland, along with Poland, had been invaded by the Soviet Union in 1940).

This is not to suggest that the fair did not bring culture to the masses, as previous fairs and expositions had before it. Vermeer's *The Milkmaid* was exhibited at the fair, as was a British copy of the Magna Carta. A French Pavilion attraction, 'Le Restaurant du Pavilion de France', would become New York's first foray into haute cuisine when it reopened as Le

Pavilion in Midtown Manhattan the next year. More surprising than Lobster à l'Américaine were the lobsters of Salvador Dalí, who, in an act of extraordinary daring, was given his own pavilion. Dalí's *Dream of Venus* featured semi-nude underwater swimmers known as the 'Living Liquid Ladies', as well as women dressed as lobsters, pianos and other pet Surrealist motifs. The fair's daring did not cross the colour line, however: the contributions of non-white artists and performers were limited to the commissioning of William Grant Still, an African American composer, to write the theme for 'Democracity', and an invitation to the celebrated contralto Marian Anderson (who had only recently made the news for being denied the use of segregated Constitution Hall in Washington, DC). Without question, the World's Fair was geared to a white audience by white organizers.

But the canned 'future' of the 'World of Tomorrow' had nothing on the rapid-fire transformations taking place in the city, visible on the Flushing Meadows horizon. New York – and New Yorkers – were changing, diversifying as never before. With the help of WPA funding, tenements made way for working and middle-class housing developments, such as real-estate mogul Fred French's 'Knickerbocker Village', a two-towered complex with a central courtyard, cooperative nursery school and active tenants association. Knickerbocker Village was urban renewal at its most showy: the buildings occupied a parcel of land on the Lower East Side once known as the 'Lung Block', a series of decrepit, slum lord-owned tenements whose residents, as Phillip Lopate points out, 'had the highest tuberculosis incidence of any street in the city'. Among the first residents of French's model housing were the alleged Soviet spies Julius and Ethel Rosenberg, first-generation Americans and young parents who lived in a three-room apartment on the eleventh floor from 1942 until the arrest in 1950 that would ultimately result in their double execution three years later. In many ways the Rosenbergs were quint-essential Knickerbocker Villagers, and typical mid-century New Yorkers, too. As we have seen, the demography of New York changed dramatically during the first half of the

The Trylon and Perisphere illuminated by searchlights at the 1939 World's Fair.

Procession of the unemployed through the streets of New York, by Achille Beltrame for the Italian newspaper *La Domenica del Corriere*, 1930.

twentieth century, and by 1950, in spite of restrictive federal immigration quotas, more than a quarter of all New Yorkers were foreign-born. Knickerbocker Village, of necessity, would have reflected this transformation of New York's population into something ever more cosmopolitan and international – more European, in many ways, than Europe itself. Joshua Freeman suggests that by mid-century, there was a 'widely shared sense, among both New Yorkers and non-New Yorkers, that New York was in the United States but not of it', and the microcosms of housing around the city surely support his claim.

New York's 'in but not of' sensibility was also reflected in the work of journalists such as A. J. Liebling and Joseph Mitchell, both of whom wrote for the *New Yorker* and other publications about the idiosyncratic people and places that made the city so inimitable. Mitchell specialized in lost causes and fringe groups such as the 'Mohawks in High Steel', members of the Caughnawaga tribe who lived in Brooklyn and worked on many of the bridges and skyscrapers around the city. The focus of Mitchell and Liebling on what might be called 'cafeteria society' as opposed to 'café society' was in step with the work of an emerging group of writers from New York's ethnic neighbourhoods who began to depict New York in their own image. Novelists such as Henry Roth, Anzia Yezierska and Irwin Shaw replaced the sentimental stereotypes of Lower East Side life that dogged popular plays such as *Abie's Irish Rose* with their own frank accounts, while Richard Wright and Ann Petry applied the tools of naturalism to the African American experience. Harlem had been hardened by the Depression, by riots and by the grinding persistence of racism, and the second wave of Harlem artists focused on the goal of equal rights with a fierce attention. The narrator of Petry's best-selling novel *The Street* (1946) captures the battle mentality of the era in the palpable relief of African Americans getting off the subway in Harlem: 'She noticed that . . . [the] same people who had made themselves small on the train, even on the platform, suddenly grew so large they could hardly get up the stairs to the street together.' Petry's New Yorkers, like Henry Roth's, live in New York, but are not considered to be part of it: they belong to their corners, their blocks and their neighbourhoods.

The built environment of the city itself registered this dislocation, too, as photographer Berenice Abbott's *Changing New York* project makes clear. Abbott, on assignment from the Federal Art Project (the visual arts component of the WPA), documented the transformation of the city's landmarks, industries and neighbourhoods on the eve of the World's Fair.

Some of Abbott's subjects were monuments to municipal power and philanthropy, such as the Jefferson Market Courthouse, the spire of St Mark's in-the-Bowery and the skyscraping canyons of Midtown, but others registered the city at its most heart-catchingly mundane: a news stand on Third Avenue, a wooden house in the Spuyten Duyvil section of the Bronx, a kosher butcher on Hester Street, a *latticini* (dairy) advertising 'ricotta tutta creama [sic]' on Bleecker. By the time funding for the Federal Art Project ran out in 1939, Abbott had already taken 302 photographs, the most comprehensive visual portrait of New York to date. Instead of 'Democracity', Abbott presented New Yorkers with their own city, ennobling its stoops, stores and waterfront in the process. And her unspoken concern for its passing was taken up by other city chroniclers who kept a weather eye on Robert Moses, even when they praised him for 'reviving interest in the history of the city', as did Helen Worden. 'The early American homes that fringed St Mark's in-the-Bowery are rapidly disappearing', Worden wrote in a World's Fair-era guidebook titled *Here is New York*. She laments, too, that while the 'nuns of Madonna House' saved Alexander Hamilton's Cherry Street home from destruction and restored it for the public, 'tourists seldom stray in. Few have ever heard of the little red brick Colonial house on Cherry Street.' Another author didn't even try to find history among the construction sites. 'This Guide', Mary Field Parton wrote, 'concerns itself primarily with the study of bigness . . . Little remains of the past, for New York is forever tearing down to rebuild.'

In a broadside entitled 'Ten Misconceptions of New York' and published on the eve of the World's Fair, Mayor Fiorello LaGuardia did his best to refute Manhattan's negative press and stem the rising tide of misgivings over Moses's rampant developments. He denied that the city was unfriendly, inordinately expensive, unpatriotic or snooty. He declared that the era of the sweatshop was in New York's past, as was its reputation for filth and disease. He praised the city's architecture as an 'ensemble [that] is unique and anything

Berenice Abbott, *Cheese Store, 276 Bleecker Street*, 1937. Note the anglicized spelling of 'creama'.

Fishmonger at the Fulton Fish Market, 1938. The market – and the South Street Seaport around it – were among Joseph Mitchell's favourite haunts.

JOSEPH MITCHELL

The journalist Joseph Mitchell, whom Salman Rushdie has described as the 'buried treasure' of American literature, specialized in New Yorkers who lived around the fringes of the city – and sometimes on the margins, too. Mitchell's 'human interest stories' were at bottom profoundly humane: there was nothing snobbish in the profiles he published in the *Herald Tribune* and the *New Yorker* (where he worked from 1938 until his death in 1996). These portraits covered a lot of ground: from the 'high steel' Caughnawaga people who lived in Brooklyn and built the city's tallest bridges and skyscrapers, to the genial 'voodoo doctor' of Harlem who labelled all his bewitching products 'alleged' and 'so-called' to avoid consumer disappointment (and charges of fraud), to an interview with the self-proclaimed 'King of the Gypsies' on the Lower East Side.

Mitchell, seemingly at ease in every Gotham milieu, brought lasting fame to some of the enduring institutions he described, such as McSorley's Old Ale House (which is still in operation on East Seventh Street) and Sloppy Louie's restaurant (which operated from 1930 to 1998 on the southern end of Fulton Street). Indeed, until the recent closure of the South Street Seaport Museum, visitors could even tour the decrepit Fulton Ferry Hotel rooms that Mitchell described in 'Up in the Old Hotel', his story of Sloppy Louie's and the ghosts of Seaport past. The Museum's preservation of these rooms was proof of Mitchell's lasting impact: his stories are as much artefacts of metropolitan life as any museum object, and arguably even more crucial to New York's collective memory.

but hodgepodge', and, most of all, he vehemently rejected the idea that New York's 'time as a great metropolis has passed'. New York City was about the future, LaGuardia insisted, and it would continue to 'lead the parade of cities' in every possible positive respect. 'We could afford to stop for the next twenty years and still we would be slightly ahead of the procession,' he concluded. 'But New York just can't stop. It's like flying – the city is sustained by the thrust of its forward momentum and by its speed. When the law of gravity changes, New York will stop progressing.' LaGuardia meant his grandstanding as a promise, although it may have struck some as a threat. Either way, the laws of gravity were about to change.

I n 1958 *Fortune* magazine published 'Downtown is for People', a resounding exhortation to the citizens and architects of metropolises everywhere. Take charge of your city, the author urged. Without the input of flesh-and-blood residents, development 'will not revitalize downtown, they will deaden it'. 'You've got to get out and walk', the article continued,

> Walk, and you will see that many of the assumptions on which [urban design strategies] depend are visibly wrong . . . there is no logic that can be superimposed on a city; people make it, and it is to them, not buildings, that we must fit our plans.

'Downtown is for People' critiqued the urban planning of cities from Boston to Fort Worth, but reserved its most pointed comments for several of New York's shiniest new building projects, such as the Lincoln Center for the Performing Arts, which was scheduled to break ground on 14 acres in west Midtown the following year. Surrounded by truck routes, Fordham University's brand-new Manhattan campus and 'one of New York's bleakest public housing projects', this projected 'cultural superblock' was yet another case of planners 'believing their block maps instead of their eyes'. In this case the planner being condemned was none other than Robert Moses, and his critic was the journalist Jane Jacobs. Jacobs, a Greenwich Village resident, had clashed with Moses once before: in 1952, she had helped to lead the successful fight against his plan to extend Fifth Avenue through Washington Square Park. But

Mayor Robert Wagner (right), Robert Moses (left) and Frank Meistrell,
Deputy Administrator of the Housing and Home Finance Agency,
on a housing project tour, 1956.

Jane Jacobs holds up documentary evidence at a press conference, December 1961.

now the stakes were much higher. According to Jacobs, the very soul of the city hung in the balance.

New York at the time of Jane Jacobs's writing was having the Rip Van Winkle moment that Moses had predicted before the World's Fair of 1939, but it wasn't turning out quite as the longtime Parks Commissioner had expected. The city was awakening all at once to a realization of its unique built environment and pluralistic street culture – and to the fragility of both. It may be a coincidence that the publication in 1961 of Jane Jacobs's most famous book, *The Death and Life of Great American Cities*, took place the same year that New York City mayor Robert Wagner created the Committee for the Preservation of Structures of Historic and Esthetic Importance (a predecessor to the current Landmarks Preservation Commission), but it is hardly a surprise. New Yorkers had discovered that the source of their 'New Yorkness', their authentic sense of self, lay, in part, in the particular physical environment that was all around them. The 1960s and '70s saw the beginning of this understanding, registered in contemporary books like James Baldwin's *Another Country*, Sylvia Plath's *The Bell Jar* and Mary McCarthy's *The Group*, films such as *BUtterfield 8*, *The Apartment*, *Midnight Cowboy* and *West Side Story* and critical ethnographic studies such as Daniel P. Moynihan and Nathan Glazer's *Beyond the Melting Pot*. These disparate works presented multiple visions of New York, to be sure, but they shared an idea of the city's necessary heterogeneity. Regardless of whether or not the citydwellers being portrayed were marginalized or mainstream, they all seemed to thrive on the qualities that Jacobs ascribes to a 'great American city' – the brash energy, diverse and densely populated streets and idiosyncratic enclaves that made up her ideal 'delicate, teeming ecosystem'.

But Jacobs's book did not stop New Yorkers from arguing over what that ecosystem ought to be, or from debating which artefacts of the city's past should be preserved and which discarded to make way for the efficient, the modern and the new. It is an endless argument, but from the 1960s through to the '90s it transformed – and imperilled – the physical landscape of the city in ways that still stagger the imagination of residents and urbanists today. Shortly after *The Death and Life of Great American Cities* was published, Carnegie Hall was declared a National Historic Landmark: the intervention of violinist Isaac Stern and philanthropist Jacob Kaplan saved the Florentine building, erected in 1891, from proposed demolition. Pennsylvania Station, McKim, Mead & White's soaring, glass-and-steel temple to transit, was not so fortunate. In 1963, in the face of organized protests and briefs to the city planning commission, the 53-year-old building was slated for demolition. 'It's not easy to knock down nine acres of travertine and granite, 84 Doric columns,' a grim *New York Times* editorial observed, '. . . but it can be done.' In fact, it took three agonizing years to finish the job, during which time Mayor Wagner appointed the city's first permanent Landmarks Preservation Commission and passed the New York Landmarks Law to safeguard the city's architectural heritage against future, Penn Station-style debacles. The stories of Carnegie Hall and Penn Station – one a tale of sparing, the other of smashing –

might be said to epitomize New York City in the second half of the twentieth century. The 'preservation ball is beginning to roll after a long uphill fight', wrote Ada Louise Huxtable, the recently appointed, inaugural architecture critic for the *New York Times*, but she cautioned against premature celebration, adding 'it is not easy . . . to keep those original buildings that provide the city's character and continuity', or to incorporate them 'into its living mainstream'. If New York wanted to keep its history, it was going to have to embrace it – all of it.

'In short, will the city be any fun?' Jane Jacobs had asked in her *Fortune* piece, before urging residents to walk their own streets with curiosity and interest. The idea of urban 'fun' would become controversial just a few years later, when brand-new mayor John V. Lindsay used the word to describe the city during a transit strike that brought greater New York to a standstill in 1966. Speaking at a televised broadcast, the native New Yorker reassured his constituents that he had not lost his faith in his hometown: 'I still think it's a fun city.' The

A contemporary image of Lincoln Center, with the Metropolitan Opera House in the centre.

An abandoned car, a vacant lot and tenement apartments on Macombs
Road, the Bronx, 1964.

newspapers, full of sarcastic wonderment, immediately took up his remark and used 'Fun City' as the metropolis's new moniker for years to come. What could be 'fun' about a city enduring high crime, political unrest and labour crises of every kind? During this particularly bankrupt time for the New York economy, Lindsay's perspective was seen not as utopian, but as delusional. Between the Lindsay and Beame administrations (when the federal assistance was requested), the national reputation of New York had changed. The city, which had only legalized collective bargaining by city employees in 1958, became known for seemingly endless labour strikes – more than eleven major ones between 1960 and 1972 – which directly affected more than 230,00 municipal jobs and indirectly affected millions more. Among the consequences of these strikes was the total stoppage of all subway and bus services for twelve days (the previously mentioned Transit Workers Union strike, 1966); the threatened closure of city hospitals (nurses' strike, 1966); mountains of garbage, overrun with vermin, on city sidewalks at the height of the summer of 1968 (Uniformed Sanitationmen's Association); and raw sewage flowing into the city's inlets, creeks and bays (the American Federation of State, County, and Municipal Employees, 1971). Among the most famous of these stoppages were the United Federation of Teachers strikes of 1968, which took place after a locally controlled school in a largely African American section of Brooklyn (Ocean Hill-Brownsville) ordered the involuntary transfer of a number of white teachers and administrators. The school had been decentralized by Mayor Lindsay in an effort to increase community engagement, but the resultant strikes by the majority white teachers' union closed the schools for a total of 36 days before a settlement could be reached, and the repercussions for community and race relations in a city of ever-increasing ethnic diversity were lasting.

Time called the strike one of Lindsay's 'Ten Plagues' in a cover story of 1968, but that same year, Lindsay's much-photographed walk through Harlem on the night after the assassination of Dr Reverend Martin Luther King Jr is widely credited with deterring the kind of riots that took place in

Washington, DC, Chicago, Baltimore, Louisville and other American cities. This convergence of events could be used to illustrate Lindsay's eight years in office: he arrived as a liberal Republican with a handsome profile and an interest in civil rights, and just as quickly he became the poster boy for massive strikes and white flight. For every improvement proposed by the mayor, from bike paths and low-income housing to investigations into police corruption (the famous 'Serpico case'), there was a catastrophic reaction to meet it: new municipal taxes, blizzards, strikes, skyrocketing welfare numbers and, most critically, ballooning city debt. The New York Knicks won their first NBA championship during Lindsay's tenure, but no credit is ever given to their authentically 'Knickerbocker' mayor. In fact, he finished his second term with dismal approval ratings, his name citywide shorthand for failure, dubbed by no less than Norman Mailer (when running to replace Lindsay) 'the most maligned man in New York'. What is lost in this glib assessment is the fact that many of Lindsay's innovations (or attempts at innovations) presage the work of a much more successful mayor, Michael Bloomberg: under Lindsay's watch, the city established the Mayor's Office of Film, Theater and Broadcasting, pushed for the diversification of the police and fire departments and instituted a 'night mayoralty' which would hear citizens' complaints or concerns 24 hours a day – much as the Bloombergian call center 311 does today (see Conclusion). The same ideas, in different circumstances, with wiser counsel – and better press.

Lindsay's successor, however, did not garner better press than he did. In 1975, the news of President Gerald Ford's refusal to give the defaulting city federal assistance was met with the *New York Daily News* headline: 'Ford to City: Drop Dead'. Although the comment proved to be apocryphal (and Ford ultimately loaned New York $500 million), the sentiment was close to the truth. The city was saved from bankruptcy not by new mayor Abe Beame but by the state-appointed Municipal Assistance Committee (MAC), headed by the Lazard Freres banker Felix Rohatyn. The MAC pushed through reforms, layoffs, tuition hikes and bond sales that

Beame and his political cronies could never have achieved, but the committee could not stem the rising rates of violent crime and vandalism in the metropolitan area. 'Welcome to Fear City', proclaimed an unofficial 'survival guide' of 1977, produced by the police union as a protest against planned funding cuts and layoffs. The crudely printed guide, emblazoned with a grinning Grim Reaper, offers safety tips that play to the concerns of tourists and residents alike: from avoiding the outer boroughs altogether to staying off city streets, 'even in Midtown', after 6 p.m. 'If you must leave your hotel after 6 p.m.,' the brochure cautioned, 'try not to go out alone', and 'never ride the subway for any reason whatsoever.' 'Fear City' was not entirely hyperbole, however: it was published the same year that David Berkowitz, the 'Son of Sam' serial killer, shot or stabbed a total of thirteen New Yorkers, killing six, before his capture. It was no time to be a proud Gothamite. No wonder that the slogan of *Network* (1976), the award-winning film about the New York television news industry, was 'I'm mad as hell and I'm not going to take this anymore!' Even Woody Allen, perpetually lovesick for the city, acknowledged this painful reality in *Annie Hall* the following year: 'Don't you see the rest of the country looks upon New York like we're left-wing, communist, Jewish, homosexual pornographers? I think of us that way sometimes and I live here.' Allen wasn't exaggerating all that much: one out-of-state congressman explained his decision to veto a bailout for the city this way: 'New York has a certain overtone of sinfulness about it.' So it's likely that few listeners were surprised or particularly alarmed to hear Howard Cosell announce in the middle of the 1977 World Series between the New York Yankees and the Los Angeles Dodgers (the latter being another, bitter example of a flight from New York): 'There it is, ladies and gentlemen, the Bronx is burning.' Add rampant arson to the list of plagues, and deep sarcasm to the list of New York traits.

Regardless of whether it was Fun or Fear City, New York was also becoming an arts capital. Not just a place where art was patronized and put on display, but where it was made.

The Hotel Chelsea (also known as the Chelsea Hotel), famous for its artist residents. Arthur Miller once wrote: 'The Chelsea, whatever else it was, was a house of infinite toleration.'

The same depressed economy that drove investors and the middle class out of town created a glut of available real estate, particularly downtown, in the very neighbourhoods that Jane Jacobs was fighting to protect. There was ample space for cheap rent in Greenwich Village and particularly SoHo, which had, thanks in part to Jacobs, narrowly escaped a Robert Moses-designed elevated highway that would have ploughed through the cobblestone streets and cast-iron architecture of that historic district. The neighbourhoods below 14th Street and above Canal became an incubator, where painters, poets, composers and performers had room enough to try on increasingly avant-garde forms. The Chelsea Hotel alone played host to dozens of artists, musicians, writers and performers, many of whom bartered works of art for a room at the Victorian Gothic brick building. The luxury of cheap space also made it possible to create a new generation of enclaves – safe havens for New Yorkers who had stepped out of the mainstream, or been pushed out, whether for their sexuality, their beliefs or their creations. Whether it was Warhol's Factory, the Stonewall Inn, the St Mark's Poetry Project or CBGB, New York had suddenly become an art epicentre like never before.

The forefather of this efflorescence of artistic enclaves was the Cedar Tavern (also known as the Cedar Street Tavern), the Greenwich Village bar that served as the unofficial clubhouse of the New York School of Abstract Expressionist painters, including Jackson Pollock, Willem de Kooning and Mark Rothko, as well as Pop artist Larry Rivers and the poets Jack Kerouac, Allen Ginsberg and Frank O'Hara, who canonized the bar in his poem 'L'Amour avait passé par là':

> to get to the Cedar to meet Grace
> I must tighten my moccasins
> and forget the minute bibliographies of disappointment
> anguish and power
> for unrelaxed honesty

When the Cedar Bar relocated in 1964 it already had a rival for sheer creative capital: Gerdes Folk City, the West Fourth Street club where Bob Dylan made his New York City debut, backing John Lee Hooker on a bill of 1961. In its original incarnation, Gerdes nurtured an astonishing array of young musical talent. In addition to Dylan, who debuted his antiwar ballad 'Blowin' in the Wind' there in 1962 with the remark 'This here ain't no protest song or anything like that', Gerdes offered a stage to Joan Baez, Janis Joplin, Jimi Hendrix, The Byrds and Emmylou Harris, who reportedly also waitressed at the club. The folk trio The Roches bartended at Gerdes, and commemorated the experience with the song 'Face Down at Folk City'.

Just a few blocks from Gerdes was the Stonewall Inn, a Greenwich Village restaurant that became a gay bar in 1966: the only gay bar in the city to allow dancing, a fact that might have been made possible by virtue of its Mafia (Genovese family) ownership. The bar operated without a liquor licence or running water to clean its supply of glasses, but that did not keep it from being enormously popular with gay New Yorkers, in particular cross-dressing men and women, who were often banned from gay bars at the time by the (largely heterosexual) management. Raids on gay bars were frequent, and while the purpose was ostensibly to seize illegal alcohol, patrons of the bars were often arrested. On the night of 28 June 1969, the patrons and onlookers caught in the middle of a typical Stonewall raid fought back – spectacularly. The mainstream media played up the camp aspects of the riot: a Rockettes-style kick line, a chorus of 'We Shall Overcome' – 'Queen Power exploded with all the fury of an atomic bomb . . . the lilies of the valley had become carnivorous jungle plants', the *Daily News* exulted – but the truth was something much more profound. The events at the Stonewall Inn were the stuff of history, not theatre. Hundreds of gay New Yorkers and their supporters rioted when the arrests began, trapping the NYPD officers in the bar and hurling projectiles (including, by some accounts, a parking meter) at the windows from outside on Christopher Street. Thirteen people were arrested during the melee, but that did not keep protesters from coming back to demonstrate (violently or pacifically, as they chose) at the Stonewall Inn in numbers reaching the thousands, for nearly a week, shouting: 'Gay Power!' and 'We Want Freedom!' While the Stonewall riots were not the first gay rights protests, they are credited with bringing the question of civil rights for gays and lesbians to the attention of the nation; inspiring gay alliances and interest groups; and galvanizing the first gay pride parade

Stonewall Riots, Greenwich Village, 28 June 1969.

in American history, which took place on the first anniversary of the riots, in June 1970. Stonewall did not solve anything for gay New Yorkers, but it was a first step into broad daylight.

There was little daylight but plenty of gay culture at Max's Kansas City, which had opened in 1965 on Park Avenue South, the international, glam-rock city mouse to Gerdes's rootsy country mouse. From the beginning, the restaurant's clientele included artists such as Donald Judd, Robert Rauschenberg and Andy Warhol, who had sold his first soup can at an uptown gallery show titled 'The American Supermarket' just the year before. To clarify, the Pop artist sold his *painting* of soup cans for $1,500, while *actual* Campbell's soup cans, autographed by the artist, were made available for $5 apiece. Warhol co-conspirators such as the members of The Velvet Underground could also be found at Max's, when they were not performing in Warhol's 'Exploding Plastic Inevitable' variety shows, and, as at Gerdes, even the staff at Max's were future stars: Debbie Harry of Blondie was a waitress there. By the 1970s, Max's had reinvented itself as a punk haven, a favourite of Robert

Crack is Wack, mural by Keith Haring on the wall of a handball court at E. 128th St and Second Avenue, East Harlem, 1986; it has been preserved and can be seen there today.

KEITH HARING

Jean-Michel Basquiat may have commanded the attention of New York's gallerists and press, but Keith Haring engaged the most thoughtfully with the texture of the city. The Pennsylvania native came to New York to study at the School of Visual Arts and soon became immersed in the city's club scene, finding like minds among the non-traditional artists Basquiat, Kenny Scharf and Futura 2000 – and taking inspiration from the graffiti that he saw all around him on city streets. While still an SVA student, Haring began to work in the graffiti form, and the result would become one of his signature genres: antic chalk drawings on the blank (and conveniently black) advertising panels in subway stations. Some of these drawings had political messages, others questioned the efficacy of religion or technology, and still others seemed like wordless exhortations to love.

Haring also created more enduring street art, in particular the brightly coloured, impish murals in city parks, pools and hospitals that can still be seen today. One of the most famous of these is the dayglo orange 'Crack is Wack' mural on the handball court at Second Avenue and East 127th Street in East Harlem, which is visible from the Harlem River Drive. The mural was completed in 1986 without city permission, but was quickly adopted by the community (and restored by the city, with the help of the Keith Haring Foundation, in 1995). The ballfields in which Haring's piece can be found have since been renamed the 'Crack is Wack Playground' by the NYC Parks Department.

Mapplethorpe, Brice Marden and Patti Smith and home to
the Misfits and the Ramones. Both Smith and the Ramones
could also be found (along with Talking Heads, among many
others) at CBGB (which stood for Country, Bluegrass and
Blues, but more often featured New Wave, punk and, later,
hardcore bands) on the Bowery. 'CBGB was the ideal place to
sound a clarion call,' Smith wrote in her memoir, *Just Kids*.
'It was a club on the streets of the downtrodden that drew
a strange breed who welcomed artists yet unsung. The only
thing [owner] Hilly Kristal required from those who played
there was to be new.'

To be new, however, often meant borrowing from the past,
as poet and singer Smith, a devotee of Rimbaud and Verlaine,
understood. New York's built environment made that co-
mingling possible, in ways that adhered to Ada Louise
Huxtable's mandate to bring preserved buildings into the
'living mainstream'. Artists are naturals at adaptive reuse, as
any loft resident will tell you. But adaptive reuse hardly suffices
to describe the Westbeth Center for the Arts, a thirteen-building
complex that once housed Bell Laboratories. The one-time
technology research centre in Manhattan's far West Village
was transformed into live-work spaces for artists – including
the photographer Diane Arbus and the choreographer Merce
Cunningham – in 1970, and remains a coveted, affordable
residence for creators and their families, despite the skyrocketing
rents of the far West Village. The 'living mainstream' can also
explain Club 57, an East Village performance space in the
basement of the Holy Cross Polish National Church where
Keith Haring, Cyndi Lauper, Fab Five Freddy and the B-52s
first tried out their songs, poetry and art. Street artist Haring
in particular credited the Club with giving him a community
– and the courage to try on a new identity. 'It's having one
night at Club 57 when everyone in the open reading was in
top form and everyone knows it and everyone is smiling',
he wrote in his journals in 1979. 'It's being quoted . . . as
saying "I consider myself more of an artist than a poet."'
The Mudd Club, a Tribeca storefront where Haring reported
seeing the performance artist Laurie Anderson in concert, was

another essential venue for this fresh generation of makers, and a particular favourite of artist Jean-Michel Basquiat and his sometime girlfriend, Madonna. Basquiat, like Haring, took inspiration from graffiti, layering it in a collage-style reminiscent of Rauschenberg, if Rauschenberg had worked with shredded street bills and markers. 'One or two words on a Jean-Michel contain the entire history of graffiti,' René Ricard wrote in *Artforum* in 1981, adding that Basquiat, with a wink to the gallery craze for all things 'street', had begun adding crowns with copyright signs to all his works, advertising their marketability with the faux-naivety that became his trademark.

The art of the street nurtured another art form that would satisfy Hilly Kristal's penchant for the 'new' hip hop. Hip hop was born in the Bronx, where DJ Kool Herc (otherwise known as Clive Campbell), a Jamaican-born graffiti and turntable artist, developed the fundamentals of this new genre at a series of dance parties held throughout the 1970s in his apartment building on Sedgewick Avenue. Other DJs, including Afrika Bambaataa and Grandmaster Flash, were inspired by Campbell, and his technique of looping song samples or 'breaks' (particularly funk classics and electropop) became one of the hallmarks of the genre by the early 1980s.

Graffiti on the subway, 1970s.

Other essential components of classic hip hop culture included beatboxing, rapping and graffiti – further proof of just how interconnected the city's alternative art scene had become. Like the work of Basquiat and Haring, this creative mashup grew out of a different kind of 'melting pot' from the

Mayor Ed Koch presides over the opening of the Temple of Dendur, the Metropolitan Museum of Art, 1978.

B-boys on Fifth Avenue, 1981.

one Nathan Glazer had in mind: the collision of influences, artefacts and events that made up daily life in New York. Sometimes this collision was horrifically violent: during the Koch and Dinkins administrations several brutal acts of racial aggression took place, including the murder in 1989 of African American teenager Yusef Hawkins by a white mob in Bensonhurst, Brooklyn, and the torture and sodomization of Haitian immigrant Abner Louima by a white NYPD officer in 1997. Hip hop was a way to turn anger into art for many of the earliest hip hop groups, including the Sugarhill Gang, Run DMC, Public Enemy and the Beastie Boys (a rare all-white group that had played at the last night of Max's Kansas City in 1981). By the 1980s, thanks in part to the arrival of MTV (and the show *Yo! MTV Raps*), hip hop was an international phenomenon. But its Bronx roots remained, and the genre's swift rise to global popularity could be seen as a victory for the city's most neglected borough, and even a harbinger for the future of the 'Boogie Down'.

New York, Cynthia Ozick wrote,

> means to impress the here-and-now, which it autographs
> with an insouciant wrecking ball. Gone is the cleaner-and-
> dyer; gone is the shoe-repair man. In their stead, a stylish
> boutique and a fancy-cookies shop . . . For New Yorkers,
> a millennium's worth of difference can be encompassed
> in six months.

Ozick's wrecking ball is currently swinging across all
five boroughs: at the beginning of a new century, the
metropolis is once again shrugging off the demands of history
and thwarting the desires of memory. Indeed, despite national
economic recessions, the millennium seems to have stimulated
development in New York in the forms of new construction
and adaptive reuse of old structures. For example: the New
York Times Company built a new headquarters, and its former
home on West 43rd Street became a deluxe bowling alley –
and so on. This New York habit of shedding pieces of the built
environment like so many snakeskins makes it difficult for
tourist and native alike to catch hold of the protean city and
affix a lasting identity to it. Is New York the graceful, Beaux-
Arts upper reaches of Fifth Avenue, or the dense scribble of
neon and noise that is Times Square? Do you catch hold of
the real thing in a taxi clattering down a cobblestone West
Village street, or is the impression more authentic from the
back of a gypsy cab speeding down the Belt Parkway into
Queens? What about the city's revitalized shorelines, newly
dense with bike paths and new plantings, that give the lie to

Jan Morris's 1969 remark that 'a distant glimpse of navigation lights, the remote passing of a liner from an office window . . . such is the sum of the average New Yorker's acquaintance with his port'? Some may feel that their clearest understanding of the city comes as they leave it, as Walt Whitman noted in 'Crossing Brooklyn Ferry'. Perhaps from the air is better still: the crowded archipelago growing smaller and blessedly manageable, penned in by its many waterways, a toy below the wing of a plane. The architect Le Corbusier thought so: 'When you see it from a plane, you think: Manhattan is a type-area for a

The fountain at Washington Square Park.

'Ground Zero', the site of the destroyed World Trade Center, 14 September 2001.

modern city; the range of banks sheltered from the sea has the purity of a theorem.' But from the ground, Le Corbusier finds it instead 'a fairy catastrophe, composed of vehement silhouettes'. That vehemence pre-dates the skyscrapers the critic has come to inspect, however. As we have seen, it has been part of the texture of New York for centuries, the physical manifestation of the city's particular exceptionalism – 'If you can make it here', et cetera, as Sinatra (a native of Hoboken, New Jersey) endlessly sang. H. L. Mencken described the phenomenon with brutal honesty: 'New York is the place where the aspirations of the Western World meet to form one vast master aspiration as powerful as the suction of a steam dredge.' It's not a very pretty idea, but it sounds about right, most New Yorkers would say; the city is never driven by any one ambition, but by the sum total of all the ambitions projected and imposed upon it.

Some have argued that the 11 September 2001 terrorist attacks that routed New York and shocked the world took New York's 'master aspiration' with them. To begin with, the disaster changed the city's skyline irrevocably, and faster than Ozick's 'insouciant' wrecking ball. The Twin Towers of the World Trade Center, which had been criticized as a display of 'purposeless giantism and technological exhibitionism' during their existence, were transformed into ideological semaphores by their destruction and emblazoned on patriotic bumper stickers and American flag pins. It may have been an inevitable transformation, but it was also a curious one: these sleek and leggy descendants of the Chrysler and Empire State buildings were icons of New York, first and foremost, not the United States – proof to many of the city's economic power and commercial pre-eminence throughout the world. The North Tower was the tallest building in the world upon completion, as well as the first to surpass the city's landmark skyscraper, the Empire State Building, in height. Only New York could top New York, apparently, and the towers did just that: the view from the observation deck was unparalleled, the restaurant (Windows on the World) one of the most profitable in the nation, the business address an international status symbol – even the wind gusts were stronger on the WTC plaza than anywhere else in lower Manhattan. The World Trade Center did not just improve on New York's verticality – it made the city more horizontal, too. The excavated earth from the construction of the towers was trucked across West Street to the Hudson River shoreline, where it became part of the landfill upon which Battery Park City was built – the last time the island of Manhattan has increased its land mass.

Whether loved or loathed, the towers became integral components of the symbolic architecture of the city, and their collapse was interpreted by many as a portent for the future downfall of New York and, in an extrapolation that surprised many New Yorkers, America, too. The Twin Towers became emblems of American freedom, although it was not their sleek and forbidding urbanity or their superlative-seeking dimensions that made them American, but the more than 3,000 people who died in the terrorist attacks there, in Washington, DC, and in Shenksville, Pennsylvania, that cloudless September day.

The events of 9/11 also changed New Yorkers' internal compass and put a dent in their famous confidence. The Twin Towers, whether admired or loathed, had been navigational landmarks for any person who found themselves ascending from a subway station below 14th Street. Unless you were at the lower tip of the island, these 110-storey signposts were to the south and their opposite was north. A quick glance to the horizon and you were on your way: no need to ask directions, thank heavens. Without the towers, Manhattanites were, if not rudderless, then a bit adrift, tourist-like. They also found it hard to navigate around their unasked-for new landmark, Ground Zero: for starters, it seemed downright galactic, more like a crater made by an asteroid than a construction site. Had the World Trade Center really been that big, the slurry wall that deep? The psychological impact of the attacks must not be discounted, either: the scale of the horror seemed to grow with the passing of time, even as the acrid odour and thick white dust at Ground Zero receded, and the frantic and mostly futile missing persons posters taped to every bus shelter and lamppost were torn down or disintegrated in the winter weather. The cataloguing of human remains that began on 12 September 2001 continues even today: new fragments of people and their belongings are still being discovered on the rooftops of office towers nearby, much as the bones of Revolutionary War prisoners from the Brooklyn prison ships washed up on the banks of the East River for years after the American victory.

In addition to creating a new landmark, the attacks also anointed new heroes, particularly Mayor Rudolph Giuliani, who was in his second term at the time. While Giuliani had previously been reviled by the city's culturati for his dictatorial 'civility' campaigns and attempts at artistic censorship, and was made a tabloid punching bag after his 2000 press conference announcing his divorce (a surprise to his wife), the events of 2001 scrubbed the Brooklyn-born politician's reputation quite radiantly clean. Even his opponents admitted that Giuliani's calm and resolve in the face of this unprecedented attack was Churchillian, and this fortitude led Oprah Winfrey to dub him 'America's Mayor'. The hyperbole was not without its logic: the last time New York had been surprised by a foreign enemy on its own soil was during the Revolutionary War. While British boats blockaded New York Harbor during the War of 1812, and German U-Boats lurked off Coney Island in the Second World War, the city had not been attacked in 225 years. If 9/11 was a harbinger of acts of terrorism to come, the

U.S. looked to New York, as they had done for centuries in many matters of much less gravity, to demonstrate the best way forward. In fact, New York is still the gold standard in American counterterrorism expertise, more than ten years after the attacks. Surveillance, radiation detection, random bag inspection in subway stations and the occasional appearance of the Agents of S.H.I.E.L.D.-like, armour-plated 'Hercules' team of police officers are all part of New York life today, and will be for the foreseeable future.

The events of 11 September also charged old words about Manhattan with new and painful meaning: W. H. Auden's poem 'September 1, 1939', for example, written during the Second World War, became a prophecy:

> I sit in one of the dives
> On Fifty-second Street
> Uncertain and afraid
> As the clever hopes expire
> Of a low dishonest decade . . .
> The unmentionable odour of death
> Offends the September night.

Similarly, E. B. White's bittersweet ode to the city, *Here is New York*, spoke as easily to 2001 as it did to 1949, the year of its publication:

> The subtlest change in New York is something people don't speak much about but that is in everyone's mind. The city, for the first time in its long history, is destructible. A single flight of planes no bigger than a wedge of geese can quickly end this island fantasy, burn the towers, crumble the bridges, turn the underground passages into lethal chambers, cremate the millions. The intimation of mortality is part of New York now: in the sounds of the jets overhead, in the black headlines of the latest edition.

More recent elegies for the city, including Billy Joel's 'Miami 2017' (which was written in 1976 about New York's famous

A Spiderman impersonator at the corner of West 40th and Seventh Avenue, near Midtown Comics.

bankruptcy and blackouts), also have an eerie resonance in a post-9/11 context. What all these songs and poems share is an emphasis on the singularity of New York, even in the face of anonymous obliteration. The 'island fantasy' of Gotham has always been about nonchalant survivorship, so what's new? Or, as a Yiddish-speaking New Yorker might say, 'nu?'

After 2001, this vaunted cool became something more than a commodity – it became a kind of talisman. Selling New York was nothing new: the city exports itself everywhere, everyday, to a global audience hungry for the next movie, the next song, the next TV show, the next novel, the next video game, even the next app – anything that will epitomize and pixilate life in this famous metropolis for the delight (or horror) of those who aren't living here, too. What is more cathartic than seeing Spiderman save Manhattan? Possibly watching Manhattan being blown up by aliens, or destroyed by a CGI tsunami. The cinematic imperilment and rescue of the city's icons has a long pedigree: think of Charlton Heston discovering the Statue of Liberty at the end of *Planet of the Apes*. Special effects notwithstanding, these movie portraits are just gaslight literature for the LED age: as this book has shown, the distillation of New York has been a business and a pastime since the nineteenth century. But the tone has changed: since 9/11 the city's self-portrait has grown darker and more defensive. Nostalgia is not the same as mourning. Life 'in the shadow of no towers', to quote cartoonist Art Spiegelman, is the real Fear City.

This shift in the New York vernacular – in its self-conscious gestalt – is evident in the literature written about or set in post-9/11 New York, much of which takes a post-apocalyptic view of the metropolis: Jonathan Lethem's *Chronic City*, for example, offers an alternate, slightly magical Gotham where tigers run amok through the Second Avenue subway line, while Michael Cunningham's *Specimen Days* finds 'children's crusade' suicide bombers spouting Walt Whitman before detonation. Both books suggest that some innocence, or perhaps arrogance, has been lost in the city: the cultural capital that once sustained a professional 'New Yorker' will no longer suffice, because some piece of that former New York is missing. *Specimen Days* brings this to life by predicting a future Manhattan that has been turned into a giant theme park, 'Old New York', where tourists pay extra for simulated muggings in Central Park and 'period dress' is required at all times, including for the 'day-shift derelict' on the imitation Bowery. 'Only a few sticklers and historical nuts wanted subway rides,' Cunningham's narrator explains, 'and then only for short distances.' In Pete Hamill's 2003 novel *Forever*, the eighteenth-century protagonist is granted eternal life so long as he never steps foot off the island of Manhattan, and instead is an eyewitness to all of the city's historic events, from the Revolutionary War and the Draft Riots to the Great Depression and the attacks on 11 September. 'You are a New Yorker', Colson Whitehead wrote in his collection of essays entitled *The Colossus of New York* (2003), 'when what was there before is more real and solid than what is here now.' This is also an apt description of Michael Bloomberg's New York.

Bloomberg, the mayor who succeeded Rudolph Giuliani, was not your typical New York pol: he was a native of Massachusetts, for starters, and a self-made billionaire who switched his party allegiance from Democratic to Republican in order to secure his first mayoral primary. He spent $73 million on his first campaign, and won. Bloomberg's mayoral inauguration was like any other: there was no portent during that ceremony to suggest that the thirteenth richest man in the world would transform New York City in unprecedented ways during his terms – which numbered three, itself an unprecedented amendment of New York's term-limit laws. 'No one since Robert Moses has so dramatically changed the face of the city,' *New York Times* editor Bill Keller wrote in the waning days of the administration, and the list of Bloomberg's accomplishments bears out the comparison to Moses – in every possible sense. Some of the mayor's initiatives radically improved the quality of life for New Yorkers, as many of the legendary parks commissioner's projects had done; these included new waterfront development, new parks (the High Line) and reclaimed parks (Governors Island). Others reduced the carbon footprint of the five boroughs, with recycling, sustainable development initiatives, bike lanes and a city bikeshare programme. Still others brought new industry to the city, including an aggressive pursuit of the motion picture industry and Silicon Valley: the creation of tech campuses (NYU-Poly in downtown Brooklyn and, soon, Cornell University on Roosevelt Island); 'green taxis' that allow livery cabs to pick up street hails in the outer boroughs, where the classic yellow taxis are scarce; and tech incubators for NYC-based startups. And, as a private philanthropist, Bloomberg's foundation routinely shored up the municipal funding doled out to the city's cultural institutions and nonprofits and launched national initiatives, such as Mayors Against Illegal Guns.

But several of Bloomberg's most high-profile mayoral programmes would, as Keller suggests, be right at home in Moses's tyrannical, 'my way or the highway' wheelhouse. The mayor pushed through citywide bans on smoking in public establishments, on trans fats (artificially created unsaturated fats) in restaurant foods and on the sale of large sweetened drinks. He pursued an aggressive 'stop-and-frisk' policing strategy that seemed disproportionately to target minority communities and drew complaints and lawsuits from civil liberties groups, even as he touted its efficacy in reducing violent crime. He placed a heavy emphasis on student test

Street art by New York-based Enzo and Nio, seen in the Gowanus section of Brooklyn.

Luxury apartments under construction in Brooklyn Bridge Park.

scores in the decision to close nearly 200 public schools and encouraged the growth of privately managed charter schools in their stead. The Bloomberg administration ended housing assistance programmes for homeless families and saw the shelter population rise to levels not seen since the Great Depression, at the same time that record rezoning and new construction made the city denser and the cost of living more expensive than ever. According to *ArchDaily*, seven of the twenty tallest buildings in New York City were built on Bloomberg's watch. And seven gargantuan buildings that were cleared for construction during the mayor's three terms will cast equally enormous (and unpleasant) shadows over all of Central Park when they are completed, the Municipal Art Society reports. The interloper from Massachusetts, some pundits grumble, wasn't able to leave well enough alone in his adopted city. But Hurricane Sandy, a 'superstorm' that hit the city (and surrounding states) on 29 October 2012, had little respect for Bloomberg's ambitions. Forty-three

'New York by Gehry', 8 Spruce Street, is the tallest residential building in New York City – and the western hemisphere. It is also the ultimate in contemporary mixed-use: the skyscraper houses luxury rentals, penthouse residences and a public elementary school.

New Yorkers were killed by the storm, thousands lost their homes, and 2 million residents spent weeks – and in some cases, months – without electricity. The painful and expensive process of rebuilding New York's coastal neighbourhoods continues today.

The election in 2013 of Bill de Blasio as Bloomberg's successor is evidence that at least some New Yorkers were

NEW YORK NOSTALGIA

Contemporary longing for New York's past is not limited to fiction: over the past decade, books, conferences, websites, blogs, walking tours and reading series have sprung up to discuss and document the lost city ('lost' being defined by each New Yorker according to their particular interests and experience) of Gotham. The luminous digital arts journal *Underwater New York* takes its inspiration from the objects found in the city's waterways and on its shores, and regularly holds live events to celebrate the art that obtains from these littoral encounters. The popular 'Forgotten New York' (a book, blog and tour series) celebrates vintage municipal infrastructure and has a section on 'street necrology' that traces old street names throughout the five boroughs. City Reliquary, a Williamsburg-based storefront museum that bills itself as 'Your Community Museum', is entirely devoted to metropolitan artefacts (including everything from tourist postcards to geological core samples) and offers space for the exhibition of New Yorkers' personal collections as well.

New Yorkers, however, are more fond of hand-wringing than of roseate nostalgia, as blogs such as 'Jeremiah's Vanishing New York: A.K.A. The Book of Lamentations' and Curbed NY's 'Gentrification Watch' demonstrate. Balance can be found at the Municipal Arts Society, which offers an extensive roster of workshops, talks and tours on urban history, city planning and the built environment, and invites New Yorkers to submit their own tours for their annual 'Jane's Walk', a five-borough celebration of the passionate activism of Jane Jacobs.

Fox's U-bet syrup, the essential chocolate syrup for authentic New York egg creams, has been manufactured in Brooklyn since 1895.

Occupy New York graffiti: a reminder to citizens, 2011.

ready for a change. De Blasio, the former Public Advocate of New York, placed his campaign emphasis on the wide economic disparities that exist in the five boroughs, and became well known for naming Bloomberg's New York 'a tale of two cities' and calling for the institution of universal pre-kindergarten programmes as a way to ameliorate the citywide income gap. He won the election in a landslide, the first Democratic candidate to be elected in nearly 25 years, and certainly the most progressive one on the 2013 ticket. It remains to be seen whether the new, Manhattan-born mayor can satisfy his perpetually dissatisfied constituents: critics note that he does not always play hardball with developers on affordable housing and suggest that more than campaign rhetoric is needed to heal the deep rift between New Yorkers and the NYPD. Many New Yorkers publicly questioned de Blasio's fitness to be mayor after he was seen eating pizza at a Staten Island restaurant . . . with a knife and fork. The media – particularly talk-show hosts – had a field day, calling the native New Yorker's bona fides into question and comparing his slice-eating style to that of another, albeit unpopular native, Donald Trump. The cutlery purportedly used by the mayor was auctioned off for charity. The *Daily News* located photos of mayors Bloomberg, Giuliani, Dinkins and even Lindsay eating pizza 'the New York way' – folded (no photo of Ed Koch folding a slice has surfaced) – the better to illustrate the gravity of de Blasio's cultural breach.

The very existence of this media event suggests that the New York swagger is not diminished, even if it has taken on a darker resonance. 'The New York Way', whether it applies to pizza, lifestyle, industry or just the art of cutting across Grand Central Terminal at rush hour, still obtains. On the 400th anniversary of the discovery of New York by Henry Hudson, the rapper Jay-Z released the song 'Empire State of Mind'. The timing may have been coincidental, but the lyrics to the 2009 ballad echo the Quadricentennial's exceptionalist spirit. To be from this particular city – to survive in this city – meant everything, 'Empire State of Mind' suggested, and Washington Irving, Walt Whitman, Maxim Gorky, Dorothy Parker, Langston Hughes, Dawn Powell, E. B.

Jane's Carousel at Brooklyn Bridge Park, flooded during Hurricane Sandy in October 2012. Fortunately, the carousel survived.

Relaxing at the Brooklyn Flea, a weekly market held in Fort Greene and Williamsburg.

White, Paula Fox and Jonathan Lethem are just a few of the native or adopted New Yorkers who would agree. 'New York is a different country,' Henry Ford once observed. 'Maybe it ought to have a separate government. Everybody thinks differently, acts differently.' There are indeed 8 million stories (8.245 million, to be precise) on the odd little archipelago of New York, and that glorious pluralism keeps the city honest, and eternal.

THE CITY TODAY

Dives and Speakeasies

While Al Capone famously observed that 'Prohibition has made nothing but trouble,' New Yorkers made that trouble glamorous. It has been 80 years since the repeal of the Eighteenth Amendment, but New York still draws on the celebrity and mystery of Volstead Act-era clubs and speakeasies to inform its cocktail culture today. This culture has come under attack, to be sure, by recent Department of Health mandates that have attempted to sanitize the famously 'dirty town' of *Sweet Smell of Success* with a citywide smoking ban and a system of letter grades for all businesses serving food (which includes many bars). Municipal reforms such as these have endangered the louche, tobacco-stained atmosphere that once characterized New York's bar scene, but they have not squelched it. Latter-day 'Thin Men' (and women) can still be found at a new generation of elegant, pitch-dark speakeasies behind unmarked doors, while the descendants of Dylan Thomas and Brendan Behan can knock back brown liquor at any number of 'dive bars' throughout the five boroughs.

As befits any New York tradition, the debate about the canon of truly authentic speakeasies and dives is never settled. There are, to be sure, still a few Prohibition-era speakeasies left, including, most spectacularly, the 21 Club, which has managed to modernize and expand its enterprise without losing its Jazz Age patina. Tourists, distracted by the toy trucks and planes hanging from the ceiling, stand elbow to elbow at the iconic bar with stylish regulars who only have eyes for their ice-cold, all-but-mandated Martinis. Newcomer and old-timer alike mostly ignore the secret of 21, which lies – quite literally – beneath their feet. In a bid to hide their 2,000 cases of contraband wine and hard liquor, the original proprietors of the speakeasy rented the basement of the neighbouring townhouse and cut an effectively invisible, 2-ton door into the solid brick wall between the buildings. A meat skewer is required to unlock the door, which is done by jiggling it with extreme gentleness through an unprepossessing chink in the brick face. Once unlocked, a cavern straight from Tolkien awaits – assuming Gollum was a vinophile. Bottles laid in by Elizabeth Taylor, Richard Nixon and Bob Hope wait for ghostly claimants. And the subterranean room where Prohibition-era mayor Jimmy Walker entertained his paramour (in order to avoid being discovered by the Feds during a liquor raid) is now a private dining room for deep-pocketed guests. Visitors without deep pockets are sometimes able to tour the cellar, too, especially if they go during off-hours – and ask politely.

Contemporary speakeasies are not quite so clandestine, but many have made a fetish out of access: unmarked doors, hidden entrances and insider information are all prerequisites. The progenitor of the current craze was a Chinatown bar called Milk and Honey, famous for its unpublished reservations line, hand-chipped ice and drinks named after regulars. In its wake

The Bar Room at the 21 Club today, complete with dangling toy planes and trucks, football helmets and baseball bats, donated by tycoons and sports celebrities.

Interior of a New York bar just before midnight on the eve of Prohibition going into effect, 1919.

came secretive (but not quite secret) upstairs venues such as the Pegu Club, a colonial-themed SoHo lair, and Angel's Share, a lounge discreetly tucked inside the Village Yokocho, a Japanese pub in the East Village. Still other postmodern hideaways can be found today inside hot dog stands (The East Village's Crif Dogs harbours Please Don't Tell, which guests enter through a retrofitted phone booth; shuttered carriage houses (Smith and Mills, complete with an absinthe fountain); water towers (the short-lived Night Heron); and sometimes simply in the dark (the funereal Death and Company, and the Raines Law Room, named after one of the legal stepping stones to Prohibition). Manhattan does not have a monopoly on the post-Prohibition speakeasy: there are more than a handful of anonymous doors in Williamsburg, Carroll

Gardens and Long Island City harbouring bartenders with handlebar moustaches and sleeve garters who mix and muddle with the grim concentration of physicists attempting cold fusion. If you don't already have an opinion on artisanal bitters, you need not apply. But the outer boroughs also lend themselves to the purest expression of the speakeasy: the police raid. In January 2013, Rotgut, an illegal bar-cum-art installation inside a Greenpoint tattoo parlour, was pre-emptively shut down in anticipation of imminent closure by the authorities. Even when liquor is legal, hidden hideaways prevail. To quote Capone again, 'you can't cure a thirst by a law.'

In contrast, New York's best dives aren't hidden on purpose, but their modesty renders them all but invisible, particularly to tourists or those in search of artisanal pours. It doesn't matter if they are, in fact, tucked away in a subway station or advertised with a glaring neon sign – only a handful of passers-by will notice them, let alone stop to peer inside. These are need-to-know establishments: those who need to know where they are, do. While the saloon that 'function[ed] as a bank, as a sanitarium, as a gymnasium, and sometimes as a home', as Joseph Mitchell once wrote, is long gone, the concept of the dive as clubhouse is not. Citywide favourites include Montero's, a former sailors' hangout on the Brooklyn waterfront where they keep only two Martini glasses on hand and the third Martini drinker must take his chances; the Subway Inn, a linoleum-tiled institution on the Upper East Side that is decorated almost entirely with images of Marilyn Monroe (the Subway Inn, set to close at the time of writing, has promised to reopen in a new – and, it is hoped, equally seedy – location); and the skinny hall-way that is Jimmy's Corner, a journalists' hangout east of Times Square where Jimmy, the boxing promoter turned barkeep, stands guard over writers downing cheap beer and free pretzels after deadline. But dive bars, by nature, are matters of opinion and defy easy classification. Must it have a pool table and a surly bartender, like the East Village's Blue & Gold Tavern? Or year-round Christmas lights like Rosemary's Greenpoint Tavern? A revolting bathroom, punk jukebox and homicidal history, like the recently departed Mars Bar? Irish bartenders and a Lotto

Subway Inn, 143 E. 60th Street.

machine, like the Punch Bowl in the Kingsbridge section of the Bronx or the Station Café in Woodside (Queens)? Consensus is impossible: the city's dive bar partisans are loyal to their particular locals and to the requirements that they meet. But all dive bar enthusiasts can agree on one thing: any bar with 'dive' in the name is not one.

New York does not lack drinking establishments: there are sports bars, hotel bars, gay bars; nightclubs, strip clubs, hookah bars; wine bars, whiskey bars, tiki bars; après-ski bars, soju bars; and even a Freak Bar, at Coney Island, where patrons can drink and mingle with performers between sideshows. Some of these possibilities are exceptional, and some even legendary, such as the King Cole Bar at the St Regis Hotel, where a charming Maxfield Parrish mural stands guard over the birthplace of the Bloody Mary, or the Algonquin, which has its own resident cat to stand guard over Dorothy Parker's spot at the Round Table. But none of these options provide the same intoxication as the city's speakeasies and dives, which by their distinctive secrecy, whether intended or not, provide the kind of intimate anonymity that New Yorkers crave.

Montero's, 73 Atlantic Avenue, Brooklyn.

Enclaves

Contemporary guides to New York often try to customize the city to the reader's particular interests. Curious about the birthplace of gay rights? Try Greenwich Village. Looking to spot an indie film star? Again, try Greenwich Village (and Tribeca). Nineteenth-century architecture, Sid Vicious, *Sex and the City* cupcakes? You might as well start in Greenwich Village. These updates on the gaslight idea of 'New York in Slices' edit the city down to a few manageable, approachable bites. It is not a balanced diet, however: there is much more to New York than what can be found below 14th Street. In particular, such guides miss Gotham's genuine enclaves: not the Garment District, the Meatpacking District or even (to borrow an old expression) the Silk Stocking District (the Upper East Side), but those pockets of real estate throughout the five boroughs where a very particular sense of community and ethnic identity still obtains.

It is possible that New York's enclaves are underpublicized because they are ever-changing. In 2011, the census recorded that 37 per cent of New York residents (3 million people) were foreign-born, and the *New York Times* reports that while New York City schoolchildren speak a total of 176 different languages, many linguists believe the city is home to no fewer than 800 languages. Given these statistics, it is not surprising to find immigrant groups shaping and reshaping neighbourhoods within a matter of decades, if not less. This phenomenon is more common in the outer boroughs, where rea-estate prices are less stratospheric and competition for commercial and residential space less fierce. The entire borough of Queens – often touted as the most ethnically diverse place in the world – serves as perhaps the best illustration: from Astoria (which

Upper Manhattan.

has been settled, in turn, by German, Greek, Bangladeshi and Latin American immigrants, among others) to Flushing (once a Quaker settlement, now home to one of the fastest-growing East Asian communities outside of Asia); but the city's other boroughs provide intriguing case studies in change as well. Bay Ridge, Brooklyn, is a classic example of an enclave with chameleonlike properties: first a summer community for wealthy Brooklynites, then the year-round home of Norwegian and Danish sailors, the neighbourhood next to the Verrazano–Narrows Bridge gained fame in the 1970s as the home of the fictional Tony Manero (John Travolta) and his Italian American family in *Saturday Night Fever*. Today, while Bay Ridge still has a strong Italian American community, it is often referred to as 'Little Beirut' after its growing population of Middle Eastern émigrés. With its many single-family homes and wide, residential streets, it can be hard to spot the neighbourhood's increasing diversity, but the presence of Greek and Antiochian Orthodox churches and a storefront mosque give clues to the presence of newer neighbours. The mix of restaurants along Bay Ridge's busy Third and Fifth Avenues is another: Lebanese and Turkish restaurants (try Tanoreen, run by a Palestinian woman who grew up in Israel) can be found side by side with temples to pasta called Vesuvio and Casa Calamari, not to mention Leske's, a Scandinavian bakery that has been turning out traditional Danish *kransekakes* and *kringles* for more than 50 years.

Similarly, the once German neighbourhood of Woodlawn Heights, in the northwest Bronx, has become 'Little Ireland', a hub for not only Irish-American New Yorkers but new immigrants as well. The Emerald Isle Immigration Center anchors Katonah Avenue, Woodlawn Heights's main drag, where the local deli does a brisk trade in Barry's Tea and the *Irish Echo* and the Prime Cuts Irish Butcher stocks meat pies and blood puddings. Even the diminutive local branch of the New York Public Library, just up the street, continues the theme with a dedicated collection of Irish history and literature. The area is named after the Woodlawn Cemetery, a verdant, nineteenth-century graveyard that is the final resting place of Irving Berlin, Duke Ellington, Fiorello LaGuardia and Herman Melville, to name just a few luminaries. But locals might be more proud of cemetery resident 'Chauncey' Olcott, an Irish-American songwriter whose credits include the popular standard 'When Irish Eyes are Smiling'.

There are many more 'Littles' among the ethnic enclaves of greater New York – including, surprisingly, 'Little Sri Lanka', in the Staten Island neighbourhood of Tompkinsville, which claims the largest number of Sri Lankans outside of that country – but few have made such a dramatic impact on the built environment of their neighbourhood as 'Little Poland', better known as Greenpoint, which occupies the northernmost part of Brooklyn, separated from the borough of Queens by the contaminated estuary known as Newtown Creek, now a Superfund site. The ironclad warship USS *Monitor* was built in a Greenpoint ironworks in 1862 and fought for the Union cause against the Confederate ironclad CSS *Virginia* in the Battle of Hampton Roads. Although today Greenpoint is best known as Williamsburg's hipster annexe, its Polish heritage is evident to anyone who visits during daylight hours. Newcomers are to be forgiven for thinking that the G train has brought them to Eastern Europe instead of northeastern Brooklyn: a forest of church steeples, from the burgundy-and-gold onion domes of the Russian Orthodox Cathedral of the Transfiguration of

Woman in 'Little Odessa' – Brighton Beach, Brooklyn.

Our Lord, to the slender spires of Saint Stanislaus Kostka Roman Catholic Church, greet commuters as they climb the stairs from the subway. The windows of grocery stores, restaurants, chocolatiers and butchers in Greenpoint are festooned with signs in Polish, and Polish is the language spoken in the shops and on the street. Of course, non-speakers will find that the staff at Sikorski Meat Market are able to guide them through their overwhelming selection of kielbasa in fluent English, although it might help to bring a Polish-speaker to place the order at the restaurant Królewskie Jadło, famous for white borscht, a Polish Easter soup that contains absolutely no beetroot at all. Some of Greenpoint's Polish landmarks have been co-opted by the young professionals who have flocked to northern Brooklyn (Greenpoint, Williamsburg and Bushwick) in search of affordable rent and studio space. These include the Polish National Home, the cavernous headquarters of a Polish benevolent association that also serves as 'Warsaw', a part-time rock venue, and the Peter Pan Donut & Pastry Shop, an unapologetically old-school doughnut emporium with classic flavours (chocolate-glazed is a must), counter service and waitresses in starched aqua-and-pink uniforms.

The enclaves of New York are almost impossible to catalogue comprehensively, in part because they are so mutable. Borough Park, Brooklyn, houses the largest Jewish population of any enclave outside of Israel and is home to more than 200 synagogues as well as a very popular kosher Chinese restaurant, China Glatt (kosher and halal Chinese restaurants are not unheard of in the major metropolitan area). Less than 6 miles away, the boardwalk of Brighton Beach (also known as Little Odessa) is jam-packed, as are its avenues, with Russian-speakers, including Georgians, Ukranians and Central Asians, as well as Russian émigrés themselves. The groceries and nightclubs of Brighton Beach Avenue cater to these expats: try Brighton Bazaar for a dizzying selection of pickles and The National for vodka and cabaret. And yet, despite the canonical reputation of both these neighbourhoods, they are also seeing their demographics diversify over time.

There remains at least one enclave on the island of Manhattan itself, a thoroughly modern reminder of a time when the entire city was mapped out in immigrant strong-holds. It is called Washington Heights, and it is home to a dense concentration of historic and cultural landmarks, including the Cloisters, the Metropolitan Museum's medieval

Produce at a Brighton Beach storefront grocery.

191st Street Station in Washington Heights is considered to be the deepest subway station in the system. The mural that adorns it is entitled *New York City is a Rollercoaster*.

collection; the Morris-Jumel Mansion (George Washington slept there); the home of actor and activist Paul Robeson; and the Hispanic Society of America, an immense, often overlooked trove of Spanish and Latin American paintings and drawings that is free and open to the public. The neighbourhood itself is a microcosm of Latin American culture: the residents of Washington Heights are largely Dominican, and the upper reaches of Broadway, Amsterdam and Sherman are filled with the sights, sounds and smells of that island's heritage. In the words of writer Junot Díaz, Washington Heights

is to the Dominican community what Miami is to Cubans, what the LES and El Barrio used to be to Puerto Ricans – the Ground Zero of our New Jerusalem, the place we settled most successfully in the wake of our diaspora.

Margot Restaurant on Broadway, in Washington Heights.

Newcomers don't have to walk far to find that 'Ground Zero': bodegas on nearly every corner tempt with tropical fruit and all the ingredients for *pasteles* (plantain and meat pies), while food trucks and *fondas* (lunch counters) offer a quick fix: try a chimichurri, a Dominican-style hamburger, from the Chimichury el Malecon truck on Sherman Avenue. Order a *sancocho* and a *morir soñando* (a Dominican-style creamsicle drink whose name translates as 'to die dreaming') from Margot Restaurant and listen for the merengue and bachata strains that are never far away in El Alto, the heights, at the island's northern tip.

Chinatowns

'Chinatown Doomed to Make Way for a Bowery Park', the *New York Times* headline proclaimed in 1907. 'Ulcer of Oriental Vice in the Heart of East Side Succumbs At Last to Progress: Joss House Sold, Gambling Curbed and Migrations from Mott Street Already Under Way.' In 1907 this bigoted prophesy would have seemed like a safe bet: surely the Chinese population of New York, limited by the Chinese Exclusion Act of 1882 (which marked the first time the United States prevented immigration solely on the basis of race), could be easily displaced – even utterly dispersed? 'The end of Chinatown is at hand', the *New York Times* insisted, but history has proven otherwise.

More than a century later, there is indeed a park 'in the heart of the East Side', but there is also still a thriving, and now many times larger, Chinatown. Columbus Park, as it was christened in 1911, sits at the intersection of the five streets that once made up the infamous Five Points neighbourhood. Instead of razing Chinatown, New York razed that earlier enclave and gave Chinatown a park. And Chinatown, in return, began (thanks to relaxed immigration starting during the Second World War) to grow in population and political clout. Columbus Park provides a kind of gateway for this new Chinatown, which lacks the elaborate pagoda gate that is a feature of its rivals in Boston, San Francisco, Philadelphia, Los Angeles, Sydney and Vancouver. Instead, New York has a sombre Second World War memorial arch perched on Chatham Square, a small green space in the middle of a seven-street intersection at the entrance to the Manhattan Bridge. Better to enter the neighbourhood

The colourful storefronts and fire escapes of Manhattan's Chinatown.

through the lively park, dodging pickup basketball games and tai chi practice, until you emerge on Mulberry Street, in front of the Fook Funeral Home, its sombre elegance a reminder that Chinatown has always been a self-sufficient neighbourhood. From Mulberry, a quick feint right on to tiny, crooked Mosco Street brings you to the Bangkok Center Grocery, the best place to get fresh curry paste and whichever brand of fish sauce you prefer. Of course, tourists in search of an immediate fix can find fast dumplings nearby (and, more crucially, a side of addictive cucumber in spicy oil) at Tasty Dumpling, but the Bangkok grocery is also a handy reminder that Chinatown's merchandise is not only Chinese, as the tourists clutching bahn mi, bubble teas and cellophane bags of Hello Kitty marshmallows unwittingly demonstrate. It's also Thai, Taiwanese, Hong Kong Chinese, Vietnamese, Filipino and, to a lesser extent, Korean and Japanese. The Chinese population of Manhattan's Chinatown is not a monolith, either: the original Cantonese population (including the nineteenth-century settlers reviled by the *New York Times*) has been joined by a burgeoning wave of Fujianese immigrants, many of whom work in an indentured capacity for some time in order to pay off their passage (whether legal or illegal) to New York.

The Fujianese community has come to dominate the social and mercantile life of Brooklyn's Chinatown, too. Sunset Park, on the edge of Green-Wood Cemetery, is a comparatively young Chinatown: the first Chinese grocery store opened on Eighth Avenue and 56th Street in 1986. Lacking the history and institutional memory of Mulberry and Mott, a visitor won't find any double-decker banquet halls or ossified (but still weirdly charming) 'Oriental' gift shops with hand-painted signs here, nor any colonial-era streets shaped like a beckoning finger (Doyers Street, home to the Num Wah Tea Parlor, the first dim sum parlour in New York). Even the temples here are slightly above street level, effectively thwarting pedestrians from gawking at people at prayer. Instead, they will find a dense commercial thoroughfare thronged with shops and busy people: choosing fruit, sizing up overstock, ordering taro buns and milk tea at the Dragon Bay bakery, reading the real-estate classifieds posted outside a variety store – entirely in Chinese. Fortune favours the attentive on Eighth Avenue: look for the man stretching, swinging and slapping lengths of dough between his fingers at warp speed and you've found Lan Zhou, the hand-pulled noodle joint that tops every food critic's list. But a non-Chinese-speaker (even an observant one) will find it a challenge to assemble a meal at Lan Zhou, or many other places in Sunset Park – most of the menus are untranslated. The low profile and rectilineal street grid of Sunset Park keeps the visitor firmly anchored in Brooklyn, however, even when the signs are in another alphabet: a quick walk across the park (there is an actual Sunset Park) brings you to the 'Little Latin America' of Greenwood Heights, while further east is Borough Park, an Orthodox Jewish community. Brooklyn's Chinatown is a shot in the arm, but not an immersive experience. That

After the confetti on a cold February day. Lunar New Year celebration, Chinatown, 2007.

requires a trip to the end of the #7 subway line: Flushing/ Main Street, in northeastern Queens.

It takes about five minutes before a new visitor to Flushing realizes that she has touched down on another continent. Within five minutes, the smell of Chinese five-spice powder has been identified on the air, and the twinkle of Flushing's sleek new banks, malls and banquet halls has been sighted through the gloaming. She has shouldered through the crush of commuters returning home, Tai Pan bakery bags in hand, and listened to (and perhaps tried to identify) the different dialects being spoken by the crowd (at least twelve). The new visitor rides unprepossessing mall escalators up to aeroplane-hangar-sized, pan-Asian supermarkets – J Mart, Hong Kong, Sky Foods, Han Ah Rheum, H Mart – their jammed shelves proof positive of the diversity of their customers. There are fruit and vegetable markets at the street level – including a branch of the Patel Brothers, a South Asian outlier in Flushing, famous for its yearly shipment of prized Indian

New Year dragons in Flushing.

mangos – but most everyone seems to do their marketing in a mall. The 'street meat' cart offers chicken hearts and lamb gizzards instead of halal. In other words, while it takes fifteen hours to fly to Shanghai, it only takes an hour to get from Manhattan to Flushing – New York's twenty-first-century Chinatown.

The cosmopolitan spirit of Flushing is in keeping with its history: the town began as a English settlement in a Dutch colony that tolerated Quakers and was the incubator, via the Flushing Remonstrance of 1657, of the American idea of religious freedom. It still is: Flushing reportedly has 40 religious institutions in one square mile, encompassing all the major faiths. It also still boasts the original Old Quaker Meetinghouse, the oldest house of worship in New York City. Flushing is home, as well, to the Queens Botanical Garden, the central library of Queens (a curvy, gleaming structure that filters in light, but not noise, from the busy street below) and, just up the street from the library, a quiet treasure: the Flushing Post Office, a mid-century building with a frieze of Art Deco murals depicting the founding of the original towns of Queens. But quiet is not the reason to visit Queens – or at least, not Flushing. There are shops to be admired (L'Affection One Stop Bridal Shop; Sharetea, the tea-and-boot shop) and banquets to be eaten (the second-storey dim sum palace, Asian Jewels Seafood). There are omnivorous quests to be made, particularly to the

Flushing Chinatown at night.

basement food court of the Golden Mall, where you'll find cumin lamb and 'hand-ripped noodles' at Xi'An Famous Foods, and, for the lawless, underground mahjong games to find. Throw your caution to the winds at the Ten Ren tea shop instead, and order a 'Taiwanese slush ice' drizzled with condensed milk and red beans. Mix, then consume in haste, before the featherlight drifts of ice have a chance to melt. This is no ordinary Sno-cone – welcome to Chinatown.

Sounds

No one need be told that New York is awash with noise. Above and below the street, the city is filled, day and night, with the sounds of dense urban living: it is an anthem of honks, screeches, whistles, shouts and crashes, played on endless repeat. The deafening results have been the subject of complaint for centuries, and cures have been offered for nearly as long. Banish carthorses, pave the cobblestones, bury subway and railway lines, regulate pushcarts, create strict 'noise codes', enforce 'quiet hours' – the sounds and their solutions change, but still the city clangs on and on. But alongside this unavoidable bassline of New York life there is a strange and often lovely melody, one that can change from street to street in ways both banal and profound. Whether they are the product of industry or of nature, these more specific sounds lend identity to New York's neighbourhoods, and provide a different kind of compass to those looking for a more idiosyncratic orientation to the city.

Whatever the song of New York City may be, it is certainly in a mixed metre. Mashups are the cliché of sound in New York, whether in Manhattan or the outer boroughs. The funereal lament of bagpipes outside St Patrick's Church will likely be answered with recorded klezmer music from a Lubavitcher mitzvah tank rolling by on Fifth Avenue. Fifty blocks south, the E-major, music-box jingle of a 'Mister Softee' ice cream truck circling Washington Square Park (by New York law, the truck is only allowed to 'play jingles' while in motion) must compete with the sounds of the park itself: NYU student classes, impromptu acoustic guitar performances and smoke breaks; the barks of four-legged socialites in the small-dogs-only run;

Fast cars and frozen treat trucks vie to make the most noise in (already clamorous) Union Square.

the clatter of vaulting skateboards; and, occasionally, a furtive enquiry, delivered in a low tone: '. . . weed?' At the northernmost end of Fifth Avenue, a different soundscape: traffic on the Harlem River Drive, which all but drowns out the gliding passage of tugs hauling scows full of scrap metal on the river itself. Once in a while, a voice like a waterfowl penetrates the din: the coxswain of an eight-man crew, giving shrill orders as they row. Across the East River, more hurdy-gurdy music, this time slightly more mellifluous than the ice cream truck: Jane's Carousel, an elaborately carved and painted merry-go-round housed in a Jean Nouvel glass box on the water's edge of Brooklyn. The carousel's gleaming hangar muffles but does not extinguish the sonic boom of the subways running over the Manhattan Bridge, 135 feet above, or the *basso profundo* blast of the Staten Island Ferry's departing horn, across the river. In parts of every borough except Staten Island, street life sounds compete not with boats but with the rattle of the elevated train, which gives a metallic backbeat to the Dominican pop, Russian techno or Bollywood ballads spilling out of the storefronts and clubs below, as well as to the hundreds of church bells that reliably mark the masses throughout the five boroughs.

Some of New York's noises follow the crowds: where there are commuting New Yorkers, you'll find subway-platform steel drum or pickle-tub players, garbled loudspeaker messages, mariachi bands hopping nimbly from train car to train car, missionaries offering words of redemption, shrieking children on a field trip, crashing purposefully into one

Breakdancing in front of the New York Public Library's flagship building at Fifth Avenue and 42nd Street.

Singer-songwriter Milton and his band performing as part of the Madison Square Park Summer Concert Series, which is held throughout the five boroughs each year.

another as their train takes a corner. Wherever tourists gather, you will find troupes of teenage breakdancers with boomboxes, 'street meat' vendors taking orders ('you want white sauce . . . withat?') observation-deck hucksters speed-selling their skyline views and cut-rate watch and wallet dealers shouting in the lingua franca of the city: 'fivedollar fivedollar fivedollar' before melting away in a twinkling, leaving only empty sidewalk behind. In more industrial areas, tracking sound will sometimes lead the listener to raging house parties, held in empty houses, and pool parties, held in empty pools. Sometimes these sounds breach the city's official 'quiet zones', which include the plaza in front of the New York Public Library (a reliably tranquil place inside, despite its marble upholstery) and Strawberry Fields, a memorial to John Lennon in Central Park. Central Park has eight 'quiet zones' in all, including Bethesda Terrace, where the plashing of the beatific Angel of the Waters fountain is often drowned out by horn players practising in the arcade under the Terrace's arches, risking a fine for the spectacular acoustics. Brooklyn's Prospect Park, on the other hand, welcomes amateur musicians with a formal 'Drummer's

Grove', where an African drum circle can reliably be found every Sunday in fine weather, and serves as a metronome for the runners, cyclists and horseback riders going around and around the park drive.

At New York's beaches, the soundtrack is more insistent and more layered. It is the Atlantic Ocean, the whistles of lifeguards, radio salsa from the boardwalk and, everywhere, the jets leaving from or landing at the city's two Queens airports. At Coney Island, add Go-Kart motors, the skeletal wooden rattle of the ancient Cyclone roller coaster and the pre-recorded come-ons from the 'Sideshows by the Seashore' hawker, inviting sunbathers to meet the fire-eating 'Insectavora, the Queen of Kerosene'. Gentrification has auto-tuned Coney Island, unfortunately: the live spieler at 'Shoot the Freak', a seedy paintball game with a human target, lost its lease. Boardwalk strollers no longer fear being abused in comic Brooklynese by this unique 'outside talker', who proved that insult was the quickest way to incite injury: the more he heckled passers-by, the more likely they were to pay for the chance to hurt his alter ego.

But while 'Shoot the Freak' may be a memory, the sound of New Yorkers talking will never be. That sound, more than any other, defines and shapes any experience of the city. 'A New York listener does a lot of talking,' sociolinguist Deborah Tannen once wrote, and, indeed, rapid-fire, collaborative, sometimes hostile conversations (or simultaneous monologues) are the stuff of stereotype, if not urban legend. Interrupting is not only permitted, it is essential to a good New York conversation – as is speed, and, if necessary, shouting. Sometimes the shouting is even in the service of a good deed, such as the 'hey lady!' that alerts a pedestrian to her dropped glove. In the outer boroughs, the talk may be as fast, but the tone is often gentler: 'whatcanIdoforyahon?' is a standard Brooklyn storekeeper's greeting, and the traditional farewell is 'take care!' Many New Yorkers whose native language is not English have taken on (consciously or unconsciously) the linguistic mannerisms of their adopted city: one of the most famous examples being the Zabars-trained Chinese nova slicers at

Stacy Kovacs conducts Batala NYC, an all-women's Afro-Brazilian samba-reggae drumming band, in Tompkins Square Park.

Sable's, an 'appetizing' (smoked fish and prepared foods) store on the Upper East Side. 'Try a sample of our lobster salad, why not?' the slicers croon in tones of the purest Mel Brooks.

But a New York listener is also always hearing: Swedish death metal through the headphones of a fellow straphanger; a screaming break-up on the sidewalk; operatic scales from the upstairs neighbour; shouted orders at a Chinatown fish market; whispered rosaries in a church. On the Upper West Side, there is a man of unknown age and status who predicts the end of days. He shouts 'Alleluia, Alleluia!' as he walks the streets with his placard, and the sound of his keening carries as far west as Riverside Park. It is comforting and unsettling in equal measure. It is also, for a corner of New York, something familiar and constant: for the song of the city, it's a local refrain.

Parks

The Children's Magical Garden de Carmen Rubio, at the corner of Norfolk and Stanton Streets on the Lower East Side, isn't the most important park in New York City. It isn't the biggest, or even the smallest. It wasn't even officially administered by the New York City Department of Parks and Recreation until the spring of 2014. But it is a shining example of New Yorkers' fierce devotion to their green spaces. The garden, three abandoned, trash- and needle-strewn lots transformed by volunteers in 1982 into a leafy orchard – complete with roosters and a 'wishing tree' – is used as a children's playspace and outdoor classroom for local public schools. Threatened by real-estate developers, this modest oasis has turned into a cause célèbre, the kind that reporters and politicians thrive on. 'This garden is a treasure, we have to keep it in the community,' council member Margaret Chin told *The Villager*. Her sentiments are echoed by New Yorkers throughout the five boroughs, who display the kind of aggressive loyalty to their parks that most Americans reserve for their sports teams. This may be because while New York has over 29,000 acres of designated parkland, it also has more than 8 million people. Claim your patch of lawn (or sand or trail or forest) while you can.

While Central Park is the acknowledged queen of the city's elaborate network of parks, New York has other, hardly lesser parks whose supporters are legion. These include Gateway National Recreation Area, which at 26,000 acres spread across Brooklyn, Queens, Staten Island and coastal New Jersey is 30 times larger than Central Park. One of the most celebrated Gateway properties is the Jamaica Bay Wildlife Refuge,

The Boathouse at Prospect Park, built in 1905.

a stunningly beautiful (and tranquil) collage of woods
and marshes that is the best place to bird-watch in the five
boroughs. Prospect Park, known locally as the favourite of
its designer, landscape architect Frederick Law Olmsted, is
another excellent spot for birders: while the 540-acre park
is only Brooklyn's third largest, it functions as the borough's
unofficial hub, and is alive on fine days and all weekends with
African drummers, horseback riders, cyclists and strollers, not
to mention picnickers waiting for the 'Celebrate Brooklyn!'
series of free outdoor concerts, come the summer months. In
northern Manhattan, a park designed by Olmsted's son affords
one of the most dramatic vistas in Manhattan: Fort Tryon Park,
overlooking the Hudson River. A mile-long ribbon of elevated
railway running down the West Side of Manhattan has become
the city's favourite new park: the High Line, complete with
native plantings, has been dubbed the 'World's Longest Green
Roof'. It is also possibly the only way to legally simulate the

Exploring the 'Summer-Long Sculptures' of the 2013 Figment Festival, an annual volunteer-driven arts event on Governors Island.

feeling of flying in New York, as pedestrians on the trestled path hover over traffic and peer into apartment windows, catching glimpses of the Hudson River as the rail trail passes through Chelsea and the West Village. A different kind of energy emanates from Tompkins Square Park in the East Village; once home to squatters and police riots, it is now a peaceable kingdom of kids, dogs, *flâneurs* and onlookers, strolling by the once-ironic 'Temperance Fountain', the gift of Moderation Society president Henry D. Cogswell, without a second thought. That is not to say that Tompkins Square Park has rejected its past: the annual Howl! Festival, a series of multidisciplinary arts events named after the Allen Ginsberg poem, takes place in the park every summer. But for total outdoor immersion in the arts, it is difficult to improve on the Socrates Sculpture Park on the banks of Long Island City, Queens, which faces Roosevelt Island and the east side of Manhattan against an ever-changing backdrop of contemporary sculptures and outdoor installations by the likes of Sol LeWitt, Keith Haring, David Lynch and Catherine Opie. Socrates also offers outdoor movies in the summer: yet another reason to be on the waterfront.

Pocket parks like the Children's Magical Garden dot the city, as distinctive as the New Yorkers who visit them. The Creative Little Garden, on East Sixth Street in Alphabet City, sits on the site of a former tenement building and is now a National Wildlife Federation Habitat. The Urban Meadow, a community garden in Red Hook, Brooklyn, looks out over the long-necked cranes of the Red Hook Container Terminal, and the well-fed chickens who reside there have an excellent view of the helicopters rising and sinking over the heliport across the harbour in lower Manhattan. There is even a Harlem pocket park named after the Collyer Brothers, famous hoarders who were smothered by their possessions in 1947. The corner lot where their brownstone once sat became one of the first privately owned 'vest-pocket parks' in the United States, and now belongs to the Parks Department. While the Central Park Conservatory Garden is too large to be called a pocket park, it is certainly a neighbourhood secret: the garden, which sits

Shake Shack hamburger kiosk at Madison Square Park.

inside Central Park but is not part of it, is best entered through an imposing, gilded entry gate that once belonged to the mansion of Cornelius Vanderbilt II, where the Bergdorf Goodman department store now stands. Once inside, the 6-acre park's formal gardens encourage quiet meditation (and ornithology) rather than the hectic biking, jogging, blading and riding that can be found in Central Park proper, just beyond its fence. But perhaps the most revelatory experiences can be had in the revitalized small parks of the Bronx, where green space is at a premium and the larger parks (such as the lush Van Cortlandt, a favourite of trail runners and cricket players) can require a long subway ride. Among these small wonders is Poe Park, a 2-acre stretch in the Grand Concourse section of the Bronx on which the one-and-a-half-storey cottage residence of Edgar Allan Poe can be found. This is where Poe lived and wrote for three years, and where his young wife died of tuberculosis (they had moved to the Bronx for the fresh air). The park is also home to a stylish, contemporary visitor's centre, designed by the architect Toshiko Mori and opened in 2011, that hosts exhibitions of local art, book clubs, public programmes and a weekly green market. Five miles south of Poe's cottage is one of the borough's newest parks, a waterfront retreat called Mill Pond Park, located in the South Bronx neighbourhood of Melrose. The park, which is part of the Yankee Stadium Redevelopment Plan (new parks in exchange for the parkland used to build the new Yankee Stadium, also in the Bronx), used to be a derelict industrial site. Now Mill Pond offers visitors tennis courts, Harlem River 'beachfront' (complete with actual beach and wooden boardwalk) and a view of the filigreed railroad bridges in the distance. Edgar Allan Poe, who once remarked that the majestic vistas of the city would soon be replaced by 'nothing more romantic than shipping, warehouses, and wharves', would be pleasantly surprised.

Kayakers from the Brooklyn Bridge Park Boathouse paddling back from a trip to Red Hook, Brooklyn, with Manhattan Island in the distance.

Water

Phillip Lopate describes the shape of Manhattan Island as 'a luxury liner, permanently docked, going nowhere'. This feeling of being tethered to the land, unable to get to sea, was a feature of New York life for much of the twentieth century. New York was an island without a coast. The West Side piers that once welcomed the *Lusitania* spent most of the twentieth century crumbling or behind barbed wire, while the East Side's coves and points were cut off from pedestrians by six lanes of the Robert Moses-designed Franklin Delano Roosevelt Drive. It wasn't much easier to reach the shores of Brooklyn, Queens or the Bronx, either: with a few exceptions, they were largely reserved for municipal or industrial use, and easiest to see from the Staten Island Ferry (en route to the borough with the most beaches). Now, slowly, the city is reclaiming its shoreline, with some spectacular results.

It is tempting to suggest that circumnavigating the island is the best way to enjoy its coasts. How else can a visitor be sure to see the fabled 'Little Red Lighthouse' perched on Jeffrey's Hook just under the George Washington Bridge? Or catch a glimpse of the mysterious and deadly East River strait of Hell Gate, made famous by the stories of Washington Irving and James Fenimore Cooper and by HMS *Hussar*, a British frigate that sank there in 1780, supposedly with a cargo of gold that has never been recovered? For the intrepid, the non-profit group Shorewalkers hosts an annual 'Great Saunter' around the island every spring: 32 miles, rain or shine, extra socks encouraged. But Manhattan's shores are easier than ever to discover in smaller increments, thanks to Hudson River Park, a 550-acre park that runs from 59th Street south to Battery Park and includes every possible amenity from batting cages and a carousel to rock climbing and a trapeze school. It also includes the busiest bike path in the United States, which pedestrians cross at their peril. Brooklyn Bridge Park, on the other side of the East River, compresses some of the same programmes into a much smaller footprint: 85 acres in the shadow of the bridge, including public boating, the previously mentioned Jane's Carousel and artisanal lobster rolls. Unlike Hudson River Park, on the Brooklyn side visitors can actually dip their fingers (and their feet) in the salty estuarial water of the East River, thanks to several pebbly bays scattered throughout the park, and when a passing barge or 'booze cruise' sends a wake towards the shore, the gentle waves breaking on the shore might briefly be mistaken for an oceanfront beach – briefly.

If circumnavigation still appeals, there is a smaller, more verdant island that can satisfy the most ardent shorewalker without risk of blisters. That is Governors Island, the former military base, now partly open as a public park and easily covered on foot or by bike (after a quick ferry ride to the island from Brooklyn or Manhattan). But for visitors hoping for a chance to do their best *On the Waterfront*, New York's coastline offers plenty of challenges, minus the longshoremen. Begin by canoeing with the Gowanus Dredgers on the Gowanus Canal, a nearly 2-mile-long waterway that has just been designated a Superfund site by the US Environmental Protection Agency. The canal, which still serves as a shipping channel for deliveries of gravel and scrap metal to industries located on its banks, is noteworthy for the opaque, grey-green colour of its water, its noxious odour (stronger in warm weather) and its near-complete lack of animal life. No birds float on the surface of the Gowanus, and the only animals that have been spotted swimming in it are those that have made a wrong turn from New York Harbor into Gowanus Bay. Still, the canal intrigues residents and visitors as much as it alarms them. Despite its peculiar hue and stink, the Gowanus suggests something romantic and vigorous in Brooklyn's past – and it looks quite beautiful in the moonlight. The canal's Superfund cousin, the Newtown Creek, divides Brooklyn and Queens and has a more noble purpose: it is home to

Old pilings at Brooklyn Bridge Park, facing lower Manhattan.

New York's Wastewater Treatment Plant and the plant's spellbinding, stainless-steel 'Digester Eggs', which look as though they were taken straight from an MGM lot to the plant in Greenpoint, Brooklyn. The Digester Eggs are open for public tours once a month, but reservations are required, and the waiting list is long. Closed-toed shoes are a must.

In lieu of a Superfund site or two, true devotees of New York's coasts take to the beach – in particular Coney Island, in Brooklyn, which is more famous today for its amusements (including the shiny new rides of Luna Park) than its narrow seashore, and Rockaway Beach, in Queens. The Rockaways, as the skinny peninsula is known, comprise a diverse set of communities, from public housing projects to single-storey beach bungalows to private, gated communities, surrounded on one side by the Atlantic Ocean and on the other by the calmer waters of Jamaica Bay. The Rockaways, and their neighbouring island of Broad Channel, were all but obliterated by Hurricane Sandy in the autumn of 2012, and the turn-of-the-century character of some of the older neighbourhoods may never be fully restored. But the A train subway service has been restored, and with it comes one of the most peculiar of New York summer traditions: surfing the Rockaways. It is not unusual to see Manhattanites board

The Gowanus Canal at night, from the vantage of the Union Street Bridge.

The Mermaid Parade is a summertime tradition in Coney Island and the largest annual art parade in the United States.

the A train to Far Rockaway with a longboard tucked under their arm, prepared to take public transit to the only legal 'surfing beach' in the five boroughs. For boarders, or those who wish to rub (wetsuited) shoulders with them, the ideal place to end a day at the beach is Rockaway Taco, a brightly painted tin shack just off Beach 90, famous for its surfer cool, even in the face of hurricanes. The boardwalks may not yet be completely replaced, but the fish tacos are definitely back.

Museums

New Yorkers are fond of bragging about culture. They will boast endlessly about the exhibitions, concerts and plays they've attended, especially if they can complain about having to duck out early in order to catch another show. Invariably these are exclusive or esoteric events – the harder to get to or to discover, the more they are prized. Did it take you three subway lines to get to the Flux Factory installation in Queens? Did you find out about the film premiere at the Brooklyn Navy Yard with two hours to spare? Did you travel by bike to the dance performance on the High Line? So much the better. The status of these events is in direct proportion to their distance from Midtown Manhattan: with the exception of Lincoln Center, the farther away from the crowds at Times Square, the more authentic New Yorkers find their experience to be. The same arcane snobbery applies to the Beaux-Arts monuments along Fifth Avenue's Museum Mile: tourists go there, not New Yorkers – unless they have tourists in tow. And with good reason: these are grand, sometimes intimidating institutions, and even when they are free, they don't always feel inclusive. How can a New Yorker 'own' the Metropolitan Museum, with its more than 2 million objects? Or grapple with the Guggenheim, up the street? Better to proudly claim a fond familiarity with the New Museum of Contemporary Art, on the Bowery, or express a preference for MoMA PS1 in Queens, with its small collection and summer dance parties, over the cavernous 'original' in Midtown.

But the act of claiming ownership of one of New York's flagship museums is not only possible, it can be positively delightful. As New Yorkers who have worked in these institutions know, the best way to shrink a museum is to scale it: go upstairs. Visitors who go upstairs at MoMA will find a cool, quiet Bauhaus staircase, recreated from the original building, hung with a Calder mobile – a peaceful retreat from the crowds. Upstairs at the Metropolitan Museum you'll find a wilderness of fully realized period rooms in which every surface has been treated with the most precise attention. It is impossible not to be transported in these spaces, or to feel that their original inhabitants have just vacated them. Standing in the carved and inlaid Damascus Room, it seems likely that the marble fountain in the floor will begin to bubble at any minute, heralding the arrival of an eighteenth-century Ottoman prince, while the glowing *trompe l'oeil* instruments, cabinets, benches and pillows in the diminutive Gubbio Studiolo, a jewel-box of Renaissance intarsia woodworking, invite a visitor's touch (please try not to!). Upstairs at the massive

The iconic lines of Frank Lloyd Wright's design for the Solomon R. Guggenheim Museum are unmistakable, although some critics have argued that it is not an optimal space for art display.

The Damascus Room at the Metropolitan Museum of Art.

American Museum of Natural History, a visitor can take refuge from the dinosaurs (and their throngs of young admirers) amid their tiny cousins in the half-hidden Hall of New York City Birds – a corridor between the Hall of African Mammals and the Hall of North American Birds that lacks the drama of its neighbours, but contains delicate, taxidermied specimens of the city's avian inhabitants. In this context, the common pigeon attains a dignity that it lacks on the sidewalks of New York. The Museum of Natural History also provides unintentional comic relief at the end of an afternoon of 'museum fatigue' via the diorama 'How to Get Bitten by a Snake', in the third-floor Hall of Reptiles and Amphibians. In a small glass case decorated with sticks and rocks, tiny plastic people demonstrate unsafe practices that lead to snake bites, including, 'When climbing, put your hands in places where you cannot see a resting snake.' It's pure, unselfconscious kitsch, and not at all what you'd expect from one of the city's anchoring institutions.

Some of the secret pleasures of New York's larger museums can be found below-stairs, too: 'The Crypt', or Jaharis Galleries, underneath the Metropolitan Museum's Grand Staircase, is a low-slung, tryst-worthy place of brick and marble packed with Coptic Christian Egyptian treasures, and hardly ever occupied by other museumgoers. The charming Florine Stettheimer doll's house, a Jazz Age shrine to Modernism complete with tiny paintings by George Bellows and Marcel Duchamp, can be

The 94-foot-long model of a Blue Whale dives over the Irma and Paul Milstein Family Hall of Ocean Life at the American Museum of Natural History.

found in a dimly lit alcove on the first floor of the Museum of the City of New York – ask a security guard to help you find the room.

Another way to experience a sense of ownership over a New York museum is to choose one that has quite literally been *owned*: the historic house museum. New York has one for every interest. Looking for an immersive experience of the nineteenth century? Try the Lower East Side Tenement Museum, where tour guides walk you through the real residences of immigrant New Yorkers, or the Merchant's House Museum, which stages nineteenth-century funerals in its elegant space. Prefer to imagine life in New Amsterdam? Visit the Piers Claesen Wyckoff House in Brooklyn, the oldest structure in New York State, and take part in their fall Breuckelen County Fair. Rather commune with the ghosts of the famous? The Louis Armstrong House in Corona, Queens, looks just as it did when Satchmo died in 1971. And for family-history-seekers, the Weeksville Heritage Center is a must: a breathtaking collection of wooden houses from the nineteenth-century neighbourhood of Weeksville, a planned community of free African Americans in what is now the Crown Heights area of Brooklyn. Weeksville, which had its own churches and school, was best known as a place of refuge for African Americans fleeing mob violence after the Draft Riots of 1863.

There is no way to do justice to the hundreds of museums in New York City. Better to savour something small and miraculous: the lines of a sculpture in the garden of the Noguchi Museum in Queens, or the collection of hand-carved *santos de palos* (religious statuettes) at Museo El Barrio at the top of Fifth Avenue. New Yorkers will advise that it takes a lifetime to feel at home in their museums, so what's the rush?

Flotsam and Jetsam

New York has been endlessly filmed, hymned and limned. More anthologies have been compiled of 'New York Writing' than any other city on earth. But New York has also been written *upon*, in meaningful and lasting ways. To the observant eye, the city is a visual palimpsest, revealing its past and present in evidence both solid and spectral. This might take the form of urban flotsam: buildings and structures, sometimes all but ruined, that have been left behind from a previous era. More often than not these are industrial or commercial artefacts hidden in plain sight – the crenellated roof of an abandoned stationhouse in the Bronx, a delicate, still-working drawbridge over the toxic Gowanus Canal or a Spanish Colonial movie theatre from the silent film era, since made into a Christian tabernacle. These pieces of Gotham's past are provocative reminders of waves of progress – and decay. The city writes on itself in other ways, too: most obviously in the form of graffiti, in all its many forms, but also painted advertising murals, billboards, commemorative street signs and plaques and, of course, neon. Collectively, these writings afford visitors and residents alike a different kind of urban anthology, one devoid of editorial colour or a thick varnish of nostalgia. The written-upon city is, simply, the city in the process of becoming – itself.

One of New York's most intriguing industrial relics is also its most mysterious: the Donjon Marine Company's 'boneyard', a marine salvage site on the Arthur Kill waterway in Staten Island. More than 100 wrecked, discarded or simply retired ships can be found there, slowly rotting in the mud of the Kill. The salvage site has always been closed to the public, which

A ship at the Donjon Marine Company's 'boneyard', a marine salvage operation in the Arthur Kill waterway of Staten Island. The boneyard houses a remarkable collection of wrecked boats and, despite being off-limits to the public, has become a source of popular fascination over several decades.

has only made it more intriguing for artists, photographers, tourists and even music video producers, who have taken various illicit routes (including by water, via kayak) past the gates in order to document the skeletal remains of a motley fleet that includes tugboats, ferries, steamships and the *PC-1264*, a Second World War submarine chaser that was one of only two ships with a predominantly African American crew during the war. It is a ghostly landscape of decaying metal and wood, and the collective history of the crafts marooned there is all the more poignant for being all but inaccessible. Trespass should only be attempted by the intrepid, or by those visiting by boat: by virtue of their advanced decay, the ships function as efficient and profoundly dangerous booby traps. A safer substitute would be a field trip to Staten Island's Snug Harbor Cultural Center, where the work [and reconstructed barge studio] of John Noble, a former seaman and artist who made the documentation of this decomposition his magnum opus, is on permanent display.

Other remnants of the city's industrial past are more visible. The Domino Sugar Refinery in Williamsburg has been a prominent feature of the Brooklyn waterfront since 1882, when it was the American Sugar Company, the largest sugar refinery in the world. The plant was in operation until 2004, and the dense, low-slung complex of brick, concrete and steel buildings just north of the Williamsburg Bridge was zoned for mixed use in 2012. Prior to its redevelopment, the factory was used as the venue for the artist Kara Walker's site-specific installation *A Subtlety*, or *The Marvelous Sugar Baby*, a 75-foot-long sculpture of a sphinx, made from 35 tons of sugar. Creative Time is not the only group to use the space during this interim: guerilla photographers crept in to

The Domino Sugar Factory in its last iteration, as a public art space. The line to enter stretches down Kent Avenue, in Williamsburg.

PROTECT THE PLANTS
STAY ON THE PATH

The High Line, one of New York's newest and most popular parks, was created from a disused railroad spur that runs above the streets of the west side of Manhattan, south of 34th Street.

capture the abandoned space, and activists are petitioning the developers to lower the profile of the buildings, protect the three landmarked buildings on the site and keep the refinery's trademark yellow logo sign, which can be seen from the Manhattan side of the river. Further south in Brooklyn, advocates for another historic sugar refinery were not so fortunate: the Revere Sugar Refinery, a chrome-panelled, Buckminster Fuller-esque structure on the waterfront in Red Hook was demolished in fits and starts by a developer whose plans were thwarted by the 2008 recession.

Not every reminder of the city's commercial past has been obliterated in favour of apartment buildings, however: the High Line, an elevated public park that runs for a mile down the west side of Manhattan, was originally a freight rail line built in 1934 as part of an initiative to remove rail traffic from Tenth Avenue, a major cause of pedestrian fatalities at the time. By the 1980s, the elevated rail had been abandoned in favour of trucking, and the neglected tracks filled with rubbish and debris, their undergirdings shadowy, dangerous spaces. Today, thanks to neighbourhood activists and open-minded city officials, the High Line offers visitors a most unlikely perspective on the West Side – one or two storeys off the ground. This hovering oasis of native plants and art installations has become a kind of spine for the Chelsea and West Village neighbourhoods it once blighted, and while the architecture that it has inspired is not always authentic, the park itself seems to be entirely so.

But nowhere was the tension between city relics and real-estate developers more on display then at the 5 Pointz Aerosol Art Center, a 200,000-square-foot warehouse turned artists' studio in Long Island City, Queens, that billed itself as a curated 'collage of graffiti art'. Every available outdoor surface on 5 Pointz was, until very recently, covered with a riot of sprayed colour, including the fire escapes, the compressors on the roof – and the roof itself. The studio was established in 1993 as a preventative measure: an enormous canvas for graffiti artists who might otherwise vandalize private property. It quickly became a living museum to the form, with murals contributed by hip hop artists such as Doug E. Fresh and homegrown talent such as the Tats Cru, a storied but controversial group of Bronx-based graffiti artists that now works on commission for corporate clients (such as Coca-Cola). The shadow of gentri-fication had long hung over 5 Pointz – two towers of luxury condos were planned – but New York's graffiti community, fans of street art and longtime residents were nevertheless shocked when the building's owners whitewashed the building in late 2013. The work of two decades was literally erased overnight.

Most of 'written-on' New York happens by stealth or under cover of darkness, so 5 Pointz was a rare collaboration between graffiti and industry. This has not prevented the city from having a vibrant graffiti culture, and from embracing the work of graffiti artists after the fact, such as the East Harlem 'Crack is

Wack' mural painted illegally by Keith Haring in 1986, which the city kept, or the graffiti exhibitions that may regularly be seen at New York galleries and art museums. In order to keep ahead of this pernicious nostalgia, the city's current taggers build on this collective past to create ever more creative and improbable forms. These include paintings made from wheatpaste; scratchitti (the act of scratching a tag in glass or plexiglass, such as a subway window) stencils; collage; and decoupage. One artist, James De La Vega, works almost exclusively in simple chalk messages (sometimes motivational, often cryptic) that he inscribes on the walls or sidewalk of East Harlem and, occasionally, other neighbourhoods within greater New York. California-born Neckface, on the other hand, builds on a bathroom-wall-ballpoint style (the technical term for this is 'latrinalia') to create large-scale autographs on vertiginous surfaces, such as movie billboards. Many of the city's best-known taggers work internationally, such as movie billboards on the side of a building prominently visible from the Brooklyn-Queens Expressway. New York attracts international artists, too, like the Boston-based Shepard Fairey (known for the 'Obey' poster featuring wrestler André the Giant, and for the 2008 Obama campaign poster that read, simply, 'Hope'). But perhaps the most interesting graffiti is the one made without any paper or paint whatsoever – and New York has that, too.

One of the best places to spot non-traditional graffiti is in the Brooklyn neighbourhood of DUMBO (Down Under the Manhattan Bridge Overpass), a mixed-use waterfront district at the point where the Brooklyn and Manhattan bridges make landfall. Like Tribeca before it, DUMBO has become wealthy, residential and sanitized – at least in the areas to the east of the Brooklyn Navy Yard Industrial Corridor. This may not sound like the best backdrop for an anarchic art form, but the neighbourhood, with its mix of narrow cobblestone and brick streets, nineteenth-century factory and warehouse buildings and endless construction sites, is fertile ground for something very new. One of the most beautiful of these new styles is called green graffiti, and it is exactly that: moss. Illicit writing or images made from moss can't help but enchant on a city street, where no moss could ever hope to grow naturally: the sight of these fragile, ephemeral patches of green hints at a primeval forest, a lost Atlantis – or just a forgotten New York. The other kind of graffiti is its opposite: steel sculptures. Their most famous creator (to date) is a graffiti artist familiar even to New Yorkers who aren't fans of his work: 'Revs'. That tag, in wheatpaste, spraypaint or regular paint, can still be found all over New York City, but the artist behind it has moved on to the medium of metal. DUMBO is where you'll find Revs's

Graffiti in Red Hook reflects the prevailing attitude towards gentrification, in Brooklyn and elsewhere.

An example of a 'Revs' tag in steel.

work most reliably, bolted to the sidewalk in front of shops and restaurants (with the owner's permission, Revs insists). 'Somebody can paint it if they want,' the artist told the *New York Times* in 2005. 'It rusts. It's more interesting that way, you know?'

Spotting 'Revs' makes for an excellent treasure hunt of an afternoon, but New York's faded advertising murals are even easier to find: just look up, almost anywhere. The city's forgotten painted ads, left to slowly become translucent on the sides of homes and businesses, function as a kind of ghostly guestbook. New Yorker Frank E. Jump has collected many of these cryptic but evocative signs in his recent book, but the assemblage only sharpens the imagination. Who chalked their cues at the pool hall called Young and Schmuck? Why was there a Knickerbocker Feather Factory on the Brooklyn waterfront? And what exactly was Dr Tucker's 59 For All Pain? The palimpsestic New York past awaits your deciphering.

LISTINGS

HOTELS

The Standard
848 Washington St, NY 10014. www.standardhotels.com/high-line

Possibly the city's most voyeuristic hotel, with windows facing the High Line and guests who prefer to keep their curtains open.

The St Regis Hotel
2 E. 55th St, NY 10022. www.stregisnewyork.com

A 100-year-old Beaux-Arts hotel in the heart of Midtown whose list of famous former residents includes Salvador Dalí and Marlene Dietrich.

The Knickerbocker Hotel
6 Times Square, NY 10036. www.theknickerbocker.com

This Astor-built Beaux Arts confection in Times Square has newly reopened as a minimalist luxury hotel, more than 100 years after its founding. The birthplace of the martini, at the crossroads of the world.

The Ace Hotel
20 W. 29th St, NY 10001. www.acehotel.com/newyork

This gracious spinoff from the Portland, Oregon, original is most famous as the 'office' of a million Silicon Alley startups. Grab a coffee from the Stumptown Roasters in the lobby and eavesdrop on the 'killer apps' in progress. Don't forget your laptop.

The Nu Hotel
85 Smith St, NY 11201. www.nuhotelbrooklyn.com

One of numerous boutique hotels popping up around newly chic downtown Brooklyn, the Nu illustrates the tensions of gentrification: it is upstairs from a bail bond service, across the street from the Brooklyn House of Detention and a stone's throw from several of the city's top-rated restaurants and most expensive brownstone residences.

MUSEUMS

Metropolitan Museum
1000 5th Ave, NY 10028-0198. www.metmuseum.org

Of course the Met is chock-full of masterpieces and rare artefacts for the ages, but the largest art museum in the United States also does 'period rooms' like no other museum in the world – don't miss the Damascus Room, the Frank Lloyd Wright 'Little House' living room or the Renaissance-era Swiss Room, with its intricate carved and inlaid panelling and wooden caryatids.

Museum of the City of New York
1220 5th Ave, NY 10029. www.mcny.org

First-rate changing exhibitions on the history of the city, its culture and politics, plus the Stettheimer doll's house, which contains tiny versions of Modernist masterpieces such as Marcel Duchamp's *Nude Descending a Staircase*.

New York Botanical Garden
2900 Southern Blvd, Bronx, NY 10458. www.nybg.org

The Forest of Arden in the middle of the Bronx. In winter, this 'museum of plants' offers its charming Holiday Train Show in its conservatory, featuring model trains running among replicas of famous New York landmarks made out of twigs, sticks, bark and moss.

Morbid Anatomy Museum
424 3rd Ave, Brooklyn, NY 11215. www.morbidanatomymuseum.org

The city's newest museum is its first devoted to the 'interstices of art and medicine, death and culture'. Take in an exhibition of Victorian mourning art or, fortified by a glass of wine from the atmospheric café, learn how to mount your own specimen in one of the museum's many popular workshops.

Queens Museum

New York City Building, Flushing Meadows Corona Park, Queens, NY 11368. www.queensmuseum.org

Go for the magical panorama of New York City (as seen by day and by night), and stay for the thoughtfully curated and edgy shows of contemporary art made in Queens, one of the most diverse places on earth.

Wyckoff Farmhouse Museum

5816 Clarendon Road at Ralph Ave, Brooklyn, NY 11203. www.wyckoffmuseum.org

A diminutive Dutch farmhouse nestled in a dell – in Canarsie, Brooklyn. The oldest extant structure in New York State, and possibly the only historic house in the state that abuts an auto body shop.

Merchant's House Museum

29 E. 4th St, NY 10003. www.merchantshouse.org

A nineteenth-century home in Greenwich Village that has been preserved as a museum. Go for a period concert, 'candlelight ghost tour' or the extensive dress collection.

Brooklyn Museum of Art

200 Eastern Parkway, NY 11238. www.brooklynmuseum.org

Brooklyn's answer to the Metropolitan Museum has a well-deserved reputation for vibrant collecting and controversial exhibitions. The permanent collection is world-class and houses the Elizabeth A. Sackler Center for Feminist Art, including Judy Chicago's *The Dinner Party*.

American Museum of Natural History

Central Park West at 79th St, NY 10024-5192. www.amnh.org

There's no getting around the school groups at this iconic place, but the galleries, both old (Hall of North American Mammals) and new (Hall of Biodiversity), are worth the crowds, and the annual 'Butterfly Conservatory', a vivarium constructed inside a museum gallery, is a transporting encounter with a flight of live butterflies.

The Cathedral Church of John the Divine

1047 Amsterdam Ave, NY 10025. www.stjohndivine.org

The cathedral of the Episcopal Church in New York is a work in progress: construction began in 1892 and has not yet concluded. In the meantime, worship, art and music endure. Visit the eclectic, pluralistic chapels and shrines that line the nave, and look for the cathedral's resident peacocks in the gardens around the fantastical Peace Fountain, just outside.

SITES

Chelsea Market

5 9th Ave, NY 10011. www.chelseamarket.com

A food market in the former National Biscuit Company factory that exemplifies adaptive reuse at its best – and most delicious. Don't miss the fennel-raisin rolls at Amy's Bread, or the chocolate sea-salt caramels at Liddabit Sweets.

Staten Island Ferry

4 South St at Whitehall St, NY 10004. www.nyc.gov/statenislandferry

Skip the lines and the fees at the Circle Line and hop on a (free) Staten Island Ferry for the best panorama of lower Manhattan and a close-up with the Statue of Liberty.

Brooklyn Navy Yard

63 Flushing Ave, Brooklyn, NY 11205. www.bldg92.org

An astonishing mixed-use waterfront campus with skyline views and a storied past. Visit BLDG 92 or take a Turnstile tour to discover the Navy Yard's military and civilian history.

Pomander Walk

Between Broadway and West End Ave and W. 94th and W. 95th St in Manhattan

In a city with very few mews, this is arguably the most charming: a tiny alley of Tudoresque houses, sandwiched between pre-war apartment buildings on the Upper West Side, that was once home to the actress Rosalind Russell.

Victorian Flatbush

Western Flatbush, bounded by Prospect Park South/Church Ave to the north, Ave H to the south, Flatbush Ave to the east and Coney Island Ave to the west. www.ditmasparkcorner.com

A hard-to-find trove of grand Victorian homes on gracious properties in the Flatbush section of Brooklyn, once known as 'The Village in the City', and now surrounded by high-density neighbourhoods. A favourite of film and television location scouts.

Jefferson Market Library

425 Avenue of the Americas, NY 10011. www.nypl.org/locations/jefferson-market

It's hard to miss the spire of this Victorian Gothic building if you're walking around Greenwich Village. Stop by to admire what Ada Louise Huxtable called 'the literature of architecture' – stained glass and spiral staircases – of this gleaming 137-year-old former courthouse.

The Cloisters Museum and Gardens

99 Margaret Corbin Dr., NY 10040.
www.metmuseum.org/visit/visit-the-cloisters

The Metropolitan Museum's little sibling is one of the city's gems: 2,000 works of art from medieval Europe, tucked inside the greensward of Fort Tryon Park, high above the Hudson River.

Brooklyn Bridge Park

334 Furman St, NY 11201. www.brooklynbridgepark.org

This lively new park hugs the Brooklyn waterfront and offers magnificent views of lower Manhattan and the Brooklyn Bridge, as well as a turn-of-the-century carousel, outdoor movies, art exhibitions and free kayaking.

Harlem Meer

East side of 5th Ave, from 106th to 110th St.
www.centralparknyc.org/visit/things-to-see/north-end/harlem-meer

A tiny, picturesque lake at the northeast corner of Central Park, where waterfowl flourish and New Yorkers enjoy catch-and-release fishing, and free concerts in summer.

Park Avenue Armory

643 Park Ave, NY 10065. www.armoryonpark.org

The Seventh Regiment Armory, built in the Gothic Revival style with rooms designed by Louis Comfort Tiffany and Stanford White, is now a cutting-edge arts centre, where large-scale installations, concerts and performance art pieces take place in a 55,000-square-foot drill hall.

ENTERTAINMENT VENUES

The Bell House

149 7th St, Brooklyn, NY 11215. www.thebellhouseny.com

Funky, easygoing venue on the banks of the Gowanus. Headquarters for indie music, nerd quiz shows and chilli cook-offs.

Webster Hall

125 E. 11th St, NY 10003. www.websterhall.com

This 1886 concert venue and nightclub in Greenwich Village was once called 'The Devil's Playhouse'. The city landmark still hosts important live music events in its ballroom and studio spaces on a regular basis, as well as the occasional aerial act.

New York Public Library

Fifth Avenue and 42nd St, NY 10018. www.nypl.org

This monumental marble temple of books is also one of the best places to catch live author events. NYPL Live, Conversations from the Cullman Center and Books at Noon are just a few of its star-studded series.

Delacorte Theater

81 Central Park West, NY 10023. www.publictheater.org

It isn't really summer in New York City unless you've taken in a performance of 'Shakespeare in the Park' at the open-air Delacorte Theater in Central Park. There's nothing like seeing *A Midsummer Night's Dream*, *Hamlet* or *The Winter's Tale* under the stars, with Belvoir Castle for backdrop.

Lincoln Center for the Performing Arts
10 Lincoln Center Plaza, NY 10023. www.lincolncenter.org

This campus for the performing arts can feel overwhelming (opera, classical music, jazz, ballet, theatre and film, plus a research library), but the permanent buzz is part of Lincoln Center's charm. Ask about the Philharmonic's daytime 'open rehearsals', where you can hear that night's music for a much smaller fee.

Brooklyn Academy of Music
30 Lafayette Ave, Brooklyn, NY 11217. www.bam.org

Brooklyn's answer to Lincoln Center is as eclectic as the borough it calls home: the campus includes a Beaux-Arts opera house, a music-hall-turned-movie-theatre and a sleek complex of studios and performance spaces tucked inside a former Salvation Army building. Go for imports from Glyndebourne or the Donmar, a Laurie Andersen or Lin Hwai-Min premiere, or the latest in Brooklyn neo-soul.

Film Forum
209 W. Houston St, NY 10014. www.filmforum.org

It doesn't get any more New York than queuing up to see a restored Godard print or an obscure Thai Western at the Film Forum, which has been holding the line on curated cinema since 1970. Choose from premieres of new independent releases or addictive repertory selections – and the popcorn's pretty good, too.

Postcrypt Coffee House
Basement of St Paul's Chapel at Columbia University. Enter the campus at 116th St and Broadway and ask at the gatehouse for directions. www.postcrypt.virb.com

A free, all-acoustic folk music venue run by students in the crypt under St Paul's Chapel on the campus of Columbia University. Really. Bring a sweater and your own mug (for half-price coffee).

Cake Shop
152 Ludlow St, NY 10002. www.cake-shop.com

One of the last of the classic Lower East Side venues for indie music. Shows downstairs, cake (really) upstairs, all night long.

St Ann's Warehouse

29 Jay St, NY 11201. www.stannswarehouse.org

Theatre, concerts and performance art in a cavernous DUMBO space on the Brooklyn waterfront, with a soft spot for interdisciplinary work and monologuists. The annual toy theatre and puppet festivals are not to be missed.

RESTAURANTS

Di Fara Pizza

1424 Ave J, NY 11230. www.difara.com

It's possible to walk right past the unprepossessing Midwood storefront of Di Fara, but to do so would be to miss some of the very best pizza in New York City. You're going to have to wait for it, however: Dom DeMarco, the Neapolitan-born pizzaiolo, takes his time with every artful pie.

Buttermilk Channel

524 Court St, Brooklyn, NY 11231. www.buttermilkchannelnyc.com

The Carroll Gardens corner restaurant is known for its fried chicken and waffles, its thoughtful cocktails and the occasional surprise visit from Beyoncé and Jay-Z. Order the candied bacon and almonds while you wait for the paparazzi to show.

Malaparte

753 Washington St, NY 10014. www.malapartenyc.com

A petite, glowing Italian restaurant in the far West Village that is a good place to drink Nebbiolo, eat spaghetti alla carbonara and spot celebrities on their night off.

Oyster Bar

89 E. 42nd St, NY 10017. www.oysterbarny.com

The luncheonette at this subterranean institution in Grand Central Terminal is out of an Edward Hopper painting, and the Saloon is hapless-tourist-proof (as are the strong and accurate cocktails). Order an oyster pan-roast, as timeless as the venue.

Egg

109a N. 3rd St, Brooklyn, NY 11249, www.eggrestaurant.com

Farm-fresh cooking in a minimalist setting. You don't need a handlebar moustache or ironic shoes to feel at home in this simple, elegant Williamsburg mainstay. Breakfast and lunch only.

Veselka

144 2nd Ave, NY 10003. www.veselka.com

A 60-year-old Ukranian restaurant in the East Village that's open 24 hours a day and caters to intellectuals, actors and anarchists hankering for borscht and blintzes. Cherry lime rickeys, too.

Famous Sichuan

10 Pell St, NY 10013. www.famoussichuannewyork.com

Skip the lines across the street at Joe's Shanghai and head for this no-frills Chinatown restaurant for a fragrant whole fish with garlic and ginger, and lots of chances to numb your tongue with Szechuan peppercorns.

Hangawi

12 E. 32nd St, NY 10016. www.hangawirestaurant.com

A Zen temple to vegetarian cuisine in Murray Hill that has been a retreat for the frazzled New York herbivore for twenty years. Wear your best socks: you are requested to remove your shoes before dining.

Katz's Delicatessen

205 E. Houston St, NY 10002. www.katzsdelicatessen.com

This legendary deli is great for dinner or a late-night snack, but bring a crowd if you plan on finishing that pastrami (on rye, with mustard). Open secret: tip the counterman for an even bigger sandwich.

St Anselm

355 Metropolitan Ave, Brooklyn, NY 11211

A twenty-first-century steakhouse in Williamsburg, where everything from avocados and shishito peppers to hanger steak and lamb chops are cooked over the open grill by impressively tattooed (and genial) chefs.

BARS AND CAFÉS

BARS

King Cole Bar & Salon
2 E. 55th St, New York, NY 10022. www.kingcolebar.com

Drink a classic cocktail under the benevolent gaze of Maxfield Parrish's jolly mural of Old King Cole, which was commissioned in 1904 by Jacob Astor for the Knickerbocker Hotel.

Montero Bar & Grill
73 Atlantic Ave, Brooklyn, NY 11201

A friendly, atmospheric bar near the Brooklyn waterfront that once served longshoremen and now tolerates (but never caters to) its gentrifying surroundings. There is sometimes (free) food.

Bar Seine at the Hôtel Plaza Athénée
37 E. 64th St, NY 10021. www.arabellerestaurant.com/barseine-en.html

This romantic bar in the Plaza Athénée hotel with a colonial flair is perfect for would-be Brideshead types with an expense account or a secret to keep.

Landmark Tavern
626 11th Ave, NY 10036. www.thelandmarktavern.org

An Irish pub on the fringes of the far West Side, offering shepherd's pie, ale and single malt, with a side of history: the building is almost 150 years old. Ask about the ghosts (plural).

Dead Rabbit
30 Water St, NY 10004. www.deadrabbitnyc.com

This Financial District bar is the apotheosis of New York's current cocktail culture: vintage concoctions (punches are a speciality) in a 200-year-old building, served by bartenders in sleeve garters and accompanied by killer fries. Expect to wait for a table.

Bemelmans Bar

35 E. 76th St, NY 10075.

www.rosewoodhotels.com/en/the-carlyle-new-york/dining/bemelmans-bar

Excellent but expensive drinks offered up alongside stellar cabaret at this bar in the Carlyle Hotel, where everything happens under the watchful eyes of bunnies in a mural by Ludwig Bemelmans of *Madeline* fame.

Rolf's German Restaurant

281 3rd Ave, NY 10010. www.rolfsnyc.com

A beer garden in the Gramercy Park neighborhood that takes its seasonal decorations very seriously. Ever wanted to eat sauerbraten under a canopy of technicolour autumn leaves and branches? Bring a fire extinguisher, just in case.

Fresh Salt

146 Beekman St, NY 10038. www.freshsalt.com

A Seaport bar favoured by the crew of the tall ship *Pioneer*, as well as locals and a handful of discerning tourists, who stop in for beer, good sandwiches and an expertly made rye Manhattan.

Clover Club

210 Smith St, NY 11201. www.cloverclubny.com

Arguably Brooklyn's cocktail pioneer, this specialist in pre-Prohibition drinks (try a cobbler) is also a darling of the brunch set.

West Bank Cafe

407 W. 42nd St, NY 10036. www.westbankcafe.com

A theatre district restaurant and performance space that is a bona fide actors' hangout. Sidle up to the bar after curtain call and keep a lookout for famous regulars.

CAFÉS, BAKERIES AND SWEETS

Caffe Roma

385 Broome St, NY 10013. www.cafferomapastries.com

Little Italy off the tourist track. Sit for a freshly filled cannoli and cappuccino in the dimly lit cafe and try not to look like you're wearing a wire.

City Bakery

3 W. 18th St, NY 10011. www.thecitybakery.com

Flatiron District bi-level bakery known for sinful hot chocolate and homemade marshmallows, as well as 'pretzel croissants'. Go hungry.

Brooklyn Farmacy & Soda Fountain

513 Henry St, Brooklyn, NY 11231. www.brooklynfarmacy.blogspot.com

A classic soda fountain in a restored 1920s pharmacy in the heart of Carroll Gardens, Brooklyn Farmacy is arguably the best place to get an egg cream in New York City (fighting words). Enjoy your Sundae of Broken Dreams while listening to the lamentations of Billie Holiday. Kid-friendly, but refreshingly not kid-centric.

Sant Ambroeus

1000 Madison Ave, NY 10021. www.santambroeus.com

Sant Ambroeus has recently expanded to SoHo, the West Village and Southhampton, but for the most atmospheric *pausa caffè*, ditch your socks, tie your sweater around your shoulders and head to the Upper East Side, where an espresso at this Milanese temple is an exercise in Italian style.

Ample Hills Creamery

623 Vanderbilt Ave, Brooklyn, NY 11238; 305 Nevins Street, Brooklyn, NY 11215. www.amplehills.com

This Prospect Heights scoop shop that specializes in inventive flavours is Brooklyn's answer to Ben & Jerry's. Try the Salted Crack Caramel, or the Crossing Brooklyn Ferry Sundae with a scoop of Ooey Gooey Butter Cake vanilla.

La Churreria
284 Mulberry St, NY 10012. www.socarratrestaurants.com/la-churreria-nolita

Chic SoHo hideaway for sinful churros – delicate, deep-fried dough sticks with a side of dipping chocolate – and Spanish toasted sandwiches that are called, without apparent irony, bikinis.

Glaser's Bake Shop
1670 1st Ave, NY 10128. www.glasersbakeshop.com

An old-school, Upper East Side bakery with lace curtains and chrome trim that is regarded as one of the last places in the city to get an authentic black-and-white cookie, made (and thickly frosted) on the premises.

Hungarian Pastry Shop
1030 Amsterdam Ave, NY 10025

Storied students' and writers' hangout across from the Cathedral of St John the Divine, where the book jackets of published authors who have been fuelled by the shop's coffee and Linzertortes hang on the walls.

Mamoun's Falafel
119 Macdougal St, NY 10012. www.mamouns.com

A tiny Greenwich Village storefront that has been dishing out falafel sandwiches and other Middle Eastern fare to hungry NYU students and would-be bohemians since 1971. Ask for their proprietary hot sauce on the side.

Papaya King
179 E. 86th St, NY 10128. www.papayaking.com

New Yorkers don't know why hot dogs and papaya juice are supposed to go together – they just know that it's a tradition (and a delicious one), as is this old-school storefront on the Upper East Side.

SHOPS

Crawford Doyle Books

1082 Madison Ave, NY 10028. www.crawforddoyle.com

The ideal little bookshop, with a selection curated by independent booksellers who have none of the attitude their jewel-like Madison Ave location might suggest. They also have a small but tantalizing selection of first editions.

Jean's Silversmiths

16 W. 45th St, NY 10036. www.jeanssilversmiths.com

A hole-in-the wall vintage silver shop in Midtown that is the secret to many a drop-dead wonderful wedding present. Jean's also offers a matching service, for those with silver spoons (or other pieces) in need of rare mates.

Obscura Antiques & Oddities

207 Ave A, NY 10009. www.obscuraantiques.com

If you're in need of a Victorian prosthesis, a pickled punk or a piece of the shroud of Turin (ok, maybe not that last one), don't miss this Alphabet City curiosity shop, where the proprietors are as warm as they are knowledgeable about their macabre merchandise.

Powerhouse Arena

37 Main St, Brooklyn, NY 11201. www.powerhousearena.com

Cool books (photography, fashion, fiction) for adults and children in an even cooler DUMBO loft space, complete with church pews for in-store reading. Don't miss their live events.

Tiffany & Co.

727 5th Ave, NY 10022. www.tiffany.com

If you're after that iconic blue box, don't miss the Tiffany flagship, where you can admire priceless gems in a Woolworth's-style setting, and have any Tiffany piece (no matter the vintage) cleaned or repaired.

Black Gold

461 Court St, Brooklyn, NY 11231. www.blackgoldbrooklyn.com

Vintage records (bought and sold), taxidermy, excellent 'pour-over' coffee and vegan baked goods. This is New Brooklyn's idea of one-stop shopping.

Books of Wonder

18 W. 18th St, NY 10011. www.booksofwonder.com

Astounding independent children's bookstore offering new and classic titles, rare books and a gorgeous selection of original illustrations for sale. Books of Wonder regularly hosts star-studded author events, and is conveniently located near City Bakery.

ABC Carpet & Home

888 Broadway, NY 10003. www.abchome.com

The department store for those who shun department stores, ABC is a wonderland of exquisite, expensive trinkets, jewellery, clothing and furnishings, just off Union Square. They also have the most refined Christmas Santa in the city: expect to wait for an audience with ABC's Victorian-style St Nick.

Kalyustans

123 Lexington Ave, NY 10016. www.kalustyans.com

Indian grocery and spice emporium on Lexington Ave in Murray Hill that is world-famous for its dizzying inventory. Dried fenugreek leaves? Wood ear mushrooms? Your choice of ten different brands of ghee? They have it.

Bowne & Co. Stationers

211 Water St, NY 10038

A transporting letterpress shop in the Seaport that is the city's oldest existing business under the same name. Printer Robert Warner always has items you didn't know you coveted, from bell jars to bobble-headed grizzly bears.

Chronology

1524

Italian explorer Giovanni da Verrazzano arrives in New York Harbor, and names the region 'Nouvelle Angoulême' in honour of the home province of his patron, King Francis I of France.

1609

Henry Hudson, a British explorer hired by the Dutch, happens upon New York Harbor and the Hudson River in his search for a shortcut to Asia – but does not stay.

1624

First Dutch colonists, primarily Protestant Walloons, arrive and settle on Governors Island.

1625

The Dutch found Fort Amsterdam on the lower tip of Manhattan Island; they import the colony's first slaves, and open its first jail.

1626

Peter Minuit purchases Manhattan Island from the Lenape for 60 guilders' worth of cloth, beads, hatchets and other goods. In the nineteenth century, this sum was incorrectly calculated – and widely reported – to be equivalent to $24. The New Netherland Institute estimates it to be equivalent to $500 today.

1654

Jacob Barsimon (bar Simon), the first recorded Jewish colonist, arrives in New Amsterdam, followed by 23 Sephardim fleeing the Spanish

Inquisition. They are admitted over Governor Peter Stuyvesant's objections.

1664
Colonel Richard Nicolls claims New Netherlands for James, the Duke of York. Governor Stuyvesant surrenders without a fight, and New Amsterdam is renamed New York.

1673
The Dutch retake New York for a year, before relinquishing it to the English in exchange for Suriname, Trinidad and Tobago, among other colonies.

1689–91
Emboldened by the Glorious Revolution, German-born colonist Jacob Leisler leads a revolt in New York City and appoints himself Lieutenant-Governor. After several years, the English regain control of the city and execute Leisler for treason.

1693
New York City's first printing press, owned and operated by William Bradford, goes into business at 81 Pearl St, near Hanover Square.

1725
The city's first newspaper, the *New York Gazette*, is published.

1741
A series of fires around the city is widely interpreted as proof of a slave plot, despite inconclusive evidence. More than 150 slaves and poor white colonists are convicted of arson and conspiracy. Most are either executed or deported.

1770
The Battle of Golden Hill, often called the 'first blood of the American Revolution', was fought between New York patriots and British soldiers in lower Manhattan over several days.

1776

American forces are routed in the Battle of Brooklyn, one of the defining early engagements of the Revolutionary War. The British seize Manhattan and use it as the base of their military operations for the duration of the war.

1783

The Treaty of Paris ends the war and grants independence to the thirteen colonies. General George Washington parades his troops south from the Bronx to the Battery as the British ships leave the harbour. The anniversary of their departure is celebrated as 'Evacuation Day' by New Yorkers for the next century.

1789

New York becomes the first capital of the new nation, and George Washington is sworn in as its first president on the steps of Federal Hall, on Wall Street. A year later, the capital moves to Philadelphia.

1792

The New York Stock Exchange opens.

1799

An Act for the General Abolition of Slavery passes in New York state.

1807

Robert Fulton and Robert Livingston launch the first commercial steamboat, which plies the Hudson River waters. The same year, Washington Irving, James Kirke Paulding and William Irving Jr, writing in the pages of the satirical magazine *Salmagundi*, give New York City its first nickname on record: Gotham, after the medieval city whose inhabitants pretended to be fools to avoid paying taxes.

1809

Washington Irving publishes the satire *A History of New York* to international acclaim. The book's narrator, Diedrich Knickerbocker, becomes a household name.

1811

The Commissioners' Plan lays New York out in a tidy street grid from 14th Street to 155th Street.

1825

The Erie Canal is opened and provides the first shipping channel between the Eastern seaboard of the United States and the Midwest.

1841

Impresario P. T. Barnum opens the American Museum, where he will exhibit real and 'gaffed' curiosities for more than twenty years.

1855

Brooklyn native Walt Whitman publishes *Leaves of Grass*.

1857–8

Central Park opens on the former site of Seneca Village, a community of free African Americans and Irish and German immigrants.

1863

Passage of the nation's first Conscription Act leads to the Draft Riots, a week of protests, looting and significant violence against African Americans by white, working-class New Yorkers.

1873

A financial panic closes the New York Stock Exchange for the first time in its history and creates a four-year economic depression in the nation.

1880

The Metropolitan Museum of Art opens to the public on Fifth Avenue and 82nd Street.

1882

The first electricity plant is built on Pearl Street, under the guidance of Thomas Alva Edison.

1883

The Brooklyn Bridge – the longest suspension bridge in the world at that time – opens to the public.

1886

The Statue of Liberty, a gift from France, is unveiled on Bedloe's (now Liberty) Island.

1890

Photojournalist Jacob Riis publishes *How the Other Half Lives*, an indictment of life in the tenements and slums of New York.

1892

Ellis Island opens as a federal immigration station.

1898

New York City is formally consolidated: its five boroughs include Bronx, Brooklyn, Manhattan, Queens and Staten Island.

1904

The first underground line of the New York City subway system opens. The *General Slocum*, a passenger steamboat carrying 1,300 daytrippers, catches fire and sinks in the East River; more than 1,000 people drown due to faulty fire and safety equipment on board. This accident remains the largest single death toll in the city's history until the events of 11 September 2001.

1910

Pennsylvania Station opens at Seventh Avenue and 33rd Street, followed three years later by Grand Central Terminal at Vanderbilt Avenue and 42nd Street.

1911

A fire at the Triangle Shirtwaist Factory in Greenwich Village kills 146 people, most of them young females, working in sweatshop conditions, who were trapped on the factory's ninth floor. The New York Public Library dedicates its flagship building on Fifth Avenue.

1917

The Jones-Shafroth Act gives Puerto Ricans U.S. citizenship. Many Puerto Rican families emigrate to New York, creating *barrios* in East Harlem, the Bronx and Brooklyn.

1924

Premiere of George Gershwin's 'Rhapsody in Blue' at Aeolian Hall, Manhattan.

1925

F. Scott Fitzgerald publishes *The Great Gatsby*; John Dos Passos publishes *Manhattan Transfer*; Ethel Waters records 'Sweet Georgia Brown' and Alaine Locke publishes *The New Negro: An Interpretation*, in which Zora Neal Hurston publishes her first story, 'Spunk'.

1927

Duke Ellington begins performances at the Cotton Club, in Harlem.

1929

The stock market crashes, triggering the Great Depression.

1931

The Empire State Building is erected. Early on, it is known as the 'Empty State Building' because it lacked sufficient tenants during the Great Depression.

1934

Robert Moses is named Commissioner of the New York City Department of Parks – a position he will hold for 26 years.

1939

New York hosts the World's Fair at Flushing Meadows Corona Park. Attractions include Salvador Dalí's Surrealist pavilion, 'Dream of Venus'.

1945

The Second World War ends after the Japanese sign the Instrument of Surrender aboard the USS *Missouri*, a battleship built in the Brooklyn Navy Yard.

1947

African American baseball player Jackie Robinson begins playing for the Brooklyn Dodgers, thus effectively desegregating major-league baseball.

1958

Alvin Ailey American Dance Theater, the first black repertory dance company in the United States, has their first performance at the Y on 92nd Street.

1959

The Solomon R. Guggenheim Museum opens in a building designed by Frank Lloyd Wright.

1964

New York hosts a second World's Fair at Flushing Meadows Corona Park. A number of the landmarks of the exhibition, including a gigantic steel 'Unisphere', NASA rockets and the 'flying saucers' of the New York State Pavilion, still stand in the park.

1965

Two years after the demolition of Pennsylvania Station, the New York Landmarks Preservation Commission is established. Malcolm X is assassinated at the Audubon Ballroom, Manhattan. Max's Kansas City opens on Park Avenue South.

1969

A police raid on the Stonewall Inn, a gay bar in Greenwich Village, sparks a protest and galvanizes the creation of a gay rights movement.

1973

Dedication of the buildings at the World Trade Center. DJ Kool Herc, one of the founders of hip hop, begins to emcee house parties in the Bronx.

1975

The U.S. government declines to bail out a bankrupt New York City, and the *Daily News* prints the headline 'Ford to City: Drop Dead'. The city, with the assistance of private bankers such as Felix Rohatyn, forms the Municipal Assistance Corp to sell bonds and set the city's budget to rights, which they do by 1981.

1978

Punk icon Sid Vicious is charged with second-degree murder in the death of his wife, Nancy Spungen, in their room at the Chelsea Hotel.

1980

The Museum of Chinese in America opens in its first Chinatown location, on Mulberry Street.

1983

Trump Tower, a pink-marble-clad symbol of 1980s opulence, rises on Fifth Avenue.

1984

Wigstock, an annual drag festival, begins in Tompkins Square Park.

1986

Artist Keith Haring paints his 'Crack is Wack' mural on the handball courts of the city playground at 128th Street and Second Avenue in East Harlem.

1987

Construction begins on the first mosque in New York City, the Islamic Cultural Center on the Upper East Side.

1989

The television show *Seinfeld*, set in and around the Upper West Side, is broadcast for the first time.

1993

The *Golden Venture*, a freighter carrying 286 illegal immigrants from Fujian Province, China, runs aground off the coast of Queens.

1999

Mayor Rudolph Giuliani threatens to cut off city funding to the Brooklyn Museum of Art in an attempt at art censorship. The public backlash is immediate. Giuliani will later create a 'Decency Panel' for the purpose of regulating art that receives public funds.

2001

The twin towers of the World Trade Center are destroyed in a terrorist attack. Nearly 3,000 people perish, including more than 400 emergency workers.

2003

Mayor Bloomberg enacts the Smoke-free Air Act, which prohibits smoking in bars and restaurants.

2005

Hundreds of residents of Manhattan, Brooklyn and Staten Island independently report a mysterious 'maple syrup smell' to the city's emergency hotline. The smell is later discovered to be that of fenugreek seed processed by a flavouring company in New Jersey.

2011

Inspired by the protests in Egypt and Tunisia, the Occupy Wall Street movement organized a massive sit-in in Lower Manhattan to protest the role of Wall Street and the '1 per cent' in creating economic collapse, as well as the influence of multinational corporations over the democratic process.

2012

Hurricane Sandy brings flooding and high water that is responsible for numerous deaths, the destruction of thousands of homes and businesses and massive power outages.

References

p. 27: *Journal of Robert Juet*, transcribed from *Henry Hudson's Voyages by Samuel Purchas* (March of America facsimile series, Number 19, Ann Arbor University Microfilms, Inc., 1966; Library of Congress 66-26304).

p. 30: Jaap Jacobs, *The Colony of New Netherland: A Dutch Settlement in Seventeenth Century America* (New York, 2009), p. 2.

p. 31: 'Further Instructions for Director Willem Verhulst and the Council of New Netherland, April 22, 1625, in *Documents Relating to New Netherland, 1624–1626, in the Henry E. Huntington Library*, trans. and ed. A.J.F. van Laer (San Marino, CA, 1924), pp. 81–129.

p. 31: 'A passenger'. Peter Schaghen, *Letter to the Directors of the Dutch West India Company* (7 November 1926), Algemeen Rijksarchief, The Hague.

p. 35: Many American accounts of the city mistakenly suggest that the Dutch name for Broadway was Heere Strat or Heere Straat, an error that seems to have been passed down through centuries of New York historians. I am indebted to historian Jaap Jacobs, the author of *The Colony of New Netherland: A Dutch Settlement in Seventeenth-century America* (Ithaca, NY, 2009) and a native Dutch speaker, for this nomenclatural correction.

p. 36: Quoted in Kenneth Jackson and David Dunbar, eds, *Empire City: New York through the Centuries* (New York, 2002), p. 33.

p. 41: Daniel Denton, 'Prosperity in New York', in *A Brief Description of New York, Formerly Called New Netherlands* [1670] (New York, 1845), p. 21.

p. 41: Quoted in Michael Kammen, *Colonial New York: A History* (New York, 1975), p. 88.

p. 44: Theodore Roosevelt, *New York: A Sketch of the City's Social, Political, and Commercial Progress from the First Dutch Settlement to Recent Times* (New York, 1906).

p. 46: John Adams in Bayard Still, *Mirror for Gotham: New York as Seen by Contemporaries from Dutch Days to the Present* (New York, 1956), p. 27.

p. 46: Sarah Knight, quoted in Mark Kurlansky, *The Big Oyster* (New York, 2006), p. 65.

p. 50: 'Andrew Hamilton's Defense', in *A Brief Narrative of the Case and Trial of John Peter Zenger* [1736], quoted in *Empire City: New York through the Centuries*, ed. Kenneth T. Jackson and David S. Dunbar (New York, 2002), pp. 60, 64.

p. 52: *Journal of Lieutenant Isaac Bangs* (Cambridge, 1890), p. 57.

p. 54: David McCullough, *1776* (New York, 2005), p. 118.

p. 54: Washington, cited in Lincoln Diamant, *Chaining the Hudson: The Fight for the River in the American Revolution* (New York, 2004), p. 52.

p. 55: Letter from Col. William Douglas to his wife, 31 August 1776, collected in Henry P. Johnston, *The Campaign of 1776 around New York and Brooklyn* (New York, 1878), p. 70.

p. 57: *London Packet*, 15–17 January 1777.

p. 57: Capt. Alexander Coffin, a survivor of the prison ships, in an 1807 letter to Dr Samuel L. Mitchill, collected in *The Medical Repository*, vol. v, ed. Samuel L. Mitchell and Edward Miller (New York, 1808), p. 261.

p. 57: Still, *Mirror for Gotham*, p. 52.

p. 58: *St James's Chronicle*, 1–3 April 1777.

p. 60: John Austin Stevens, ed., *The Magazine of American History: With Notes and Queries* (New York, 1881), vols VI–VII.

p. 61: Maya Jasanoff, *Liberty's Exiles: American Loyalists in the Revolutionary World* (New York, 2011), p. 94.

p. 65: Noah Webster, in Kurlansky, *The Big Oyster*, p. 88.

p. 65: 'English visitor'. Rev. Andrew Burnaby, *Travels through the Middle Settlements in North-America, in the Years 1759 and 1760* (London, 1775), p. 95.

p. 65: Fisher Ames, quoted in Stephen L. Schechter and Wendell Edward Tripp, *World of the Founders: New York Communities in the Federal Period* (Lanham, MD, 1990), p. 7.

p. 65: Abigail Adams, *Letters of Mrs Adams: The Wife of John Adams* (Boston, MA, 1840), vol. II, p. 209.

p. 66: *Collections of the New-York Historical Society for the Year 1809* (New York, 1811), p. 13.

p. 66: Ibid., p. 9.

p. 67: John Lambert, *Travels through Canada, and the United States of North America, in the Years 1806, 1807, & 1808* (London, 1814), p. 55.

p. 71: Washington Irving, *A History of New York*, in *Washington Irving: Tales, History and Sketches*, ed. James W. Tuttleton (New York, 1983).

p. 71: 'The New York story'. It is no accident that Philip Lopate begins his excellent anthology, *Writing New York*, with an excerpt from Irving's *History*. Lopate credits Irving with creating the 'ironic, disenchanted voice' that would 'set the tone for much New York literature to come', although, in considering Knickerbocker himself 'one of history's "losers"', he misses the joyful, celebratory aspect of Irving's text and Knickerbocker's narration – an aspect which is as crucial to the Knickerbocker identity as irony. Lopate, *Writing New York* (New York, 1998), p. 1.

p. 72: Ibid., p. 80.

p. 73: Fitz-Greene Halleck, *Fanny, with Other Poems* (New York, 1846).

p. 73: Philip Freneau, 'To a New England Poet', in *The Norton Anthology of American Literature* (New York, 1989), p. 740.

p. 74: Lopate, *Writing New York*, p. 97.

p. 75: Ibid., p. 105.

p. 75: George C. Foster, *New York in Slices, by an Experienced Carver* (New York, 1850), pp. 4, 24.

p. 75: 1850 was the first year that Census data included country of origin. The change in the population of Brooklyn (King's County) was much more dramatic – from 5,700 inhabitants in 1800 to 138,000 by 1850 – suggesting that many new immigrants found their way across the East River in search of real estate (and perhaps some New Yorkers did, too).

p. 76: 'New York's tenements'. Elizabeth Blackmar notes in *Manhattan for Rent: 1785–1850* (Ithaca, NY, 1989) that the '"Five Points" tenant houses, brothels and saloons had become, to many citizens' dismay, a major tourist attraction as the center of the city's lowlife.' She points out that in his *Notes on America* Charles Dickens 'likened the Points to London's own notorious East End', pp. 179–80.

p. 79: Herman Melville, *Moby Dick* (New York, 1979), p. 3.

p. 79: Walt Whitman, 'Crossing Brooklyn Ferry', in *Whitman: Poetry and Prose* (New York: Library of America, 1982), p. 308.

p. 82: Walt Whitman, *Specimen Days*, in *Whitman: Poetry and Prose*, p. 823.

p. 82: Rufus W. Griswold, 'Review of *Leaves of Grass* (1855)', *The Criterion*, 10 November 1855.

p. 82: Walt Whitman, *Leaves of Grass,* in *Whitman: Poetry and Prose*, pp. 53–4.

p. 83: T. Addison Richards, 'New York Circumnavigated', *Harper's Magazine*, July 1861.

pp. 85–6: *Reports and Documents of the Union Defense Committee of the Citizens of New York*, Document No. 18 (New York, 1861), pp. 16–17.

p. 89: 'Marble Palace'. Stuart Blumin, *The Emergence of the Middle Class: Social Experience in the American City, 1760–1900* (Cambridge, 1989), p. 86.

pp. 89–90: *Leslie's Weekly*, 28 October 1865, p. 162.

p. 91: Rebecca H. Insley, 'An Interview with Mrs Astor', *Delineator*, 72 (October 1908).

p. 95: 'The Myth of the Four Hundred', *The Cosmopolitan*, July 1895, p. 331.

p. 98: *New York Times*, 1 January 1898, p. 2.

p. 100: Andrew Haswell Green, *Municipal Consolidation Inquiry Communication of Andrew H. Green, to the Legislature of the State of New York, Copy of Act Creating Commission of Inquiry, and Addresses of the President to the Commissioners* (New York, 1893), p. 57.

p. 107: F. Scott Fitzgerald, *The Great Gatsby* (New York, 2004), p. 13.

p. 107: Jackson and Dunbar, eds, *Empire City*, p. 400.

p. 108: Ibid., p. 451.

p. 109: Alain Locke, 'Negro Youth Speaks', in *The New Negro* (New York, 1925), p. 48.

p. 110: Langston Hughes, *Collected Poems of Langston Hughes* (New York, 1995), p. 547.

p. 111: John Dos Passos, *Manhattan Transfer* (Boston, MA, 1925), p. 112.

p. 113: *New York Times*, 5 March 1939.

p. 114: Ibid.

p. 116: Phillip Lopate, *Waterfront: A Journey around Manhattan* (New York, 2004), p. 275.

p. 120: Helen Worden, *Here is New York* (Garden City, NY, 1939), pp. 374, 376.

p. 120: Mary Field Parton, *Metropolis: A Study of New York* (New York, 1939), p. vi.

p. 124: LaGuardia, quoted in Jackson and Dunbar, eds, *Empire City*, pp. 650–52.

p. 128: *New York Times*, 30 October 1963.

p. 129: *New York Times*, 9 May 1965.

p. 135: Frank O'Hara, *Selected Poems of Frank O'Hara* (New York, 2008), p. 165.

p. 140: Patti Smith, *Just Kids* (New York, 2010), p. 245.

p. 140: Keith Haring, *Journals* (New York, 2010), p. 63.

p. 141: René Ricard, 'The Radiant Child', *Artforum*, December 1981.

p. 144: Cynthia Ozick, 'The Synthetic Sublime', in *Quarrel and Quandary*, excerpted in *Empire City*, ed. Jackson and Dunbar, p. 949.

p. 145: Jan Morris, *The Great Port: A Passage through New York* (New York, 1985).

p. 146: 'Purposeless gigantism'. Le Corbusier, 'A Place of Radiant Grace', in *When the Cathedrals Were White* (New York, 1947), pp. 87, 91.

p. 146: Lewis Mumford, *The Pentagon of Power* (New York, 1970), p. 342.

p. 149: E. B. White, *Here is New York* (New York, 2000) p. 54.

p. 151: Michael Cunningham, *Specimen Days* (New York, 2006), pp. 229, 242.

p. 152: Colson Whitehead, *The Colossus of New York* (New York, 2003), p. 4.

p. 152: Bill Keller, 'The Bloomberg Legacy', *New York Times*, 14 July 2013.

p. 165: Joseph Mitchell, 'Drunks', in *My Ears Are Bent* [1938] (New York, 2001), p. 25.

p. 173: Junot Díaz, 'He'll Take El Alto', *Gourmet*, September 2007.

p. 175: 'Chinatown Doomed to Make Way For A Bowery Park', *New York Times*, 17 February 1907.

p. 195: Lopate, *Waterfront*, p. 10.

p. 212: Randy Kennedy, 'A Graffiti Legend is Back on the Street', *New York Times*, 18 April 2005.

p. 212: Frank E. Jump, *Fading Ads of New York City* (New York, 2011).

Suggested Reading and Viewing

Fiction

Allen, Woody, *Without Feathers* (New York, 1975)

Alvarez, Julia, *How the Garcia Girls Lost their Accents* (Chapel Hill, NC, 1991)

Auster, Paul, *The New York Trilogy* (New York, 1990)

Brown, Claude, *Manchild in the Promised Land* (New York, 1965)

Chabon, Michael, *The Amazing Adventures of Kavalier and Clay* (New York, 2000)

Colwin, Laurie, *Happy All the Time* (New York, 1978)

Dos Passos, John, *Manhattan Transfer* (New York, 1925)

Ellis, Brett Easton, *American Psycho* (New York, 1991)

Ellison, Ralph, *Invisible Man* (New York, 1995)

Fitzgerald, F. Scott, *The Great Gatsby* [1925] (New York, 2004)

Fitzhugh, Louise, *Harriet the Spy* (New York, 1964)

Hammett, Dashiell, *The Thin Man* (New York, 1992)

Hardwick, Elizabeth, *Sleepless Nights* (New York, 1979)

Howells, William Dean, *A Hazard of New Fortunes* (New York, 1890)

Hughes, Langston, *Collected Works of Langston Hughes* (Columbia, MO, 2001)

James, Henry, *Washington Square* (New York, 2013)

Janowitz, Tama, *Slaves of New York* (New York, 1986)

Konigsburg, E. L., *From the Mixed-up Files of Mrs Basil E. Frankweiler* (New York, 1967)

Larsen, Nella, *Quicksand and Passing* (New Brunswick, NJ, 1986)

Lethem, Jonathan, *Fortress of Solitude* (New York, 2003)

—, *Chronic City* (New York, 2009)

McCann, Colum, *Let the Great World Spin* (New York, 2009)

McCarthy, Mary, *The Group* (New York, 1963)

McInerney, Jay, *Bright Lights, Big City* (New York, 1984)

Marshall, Paule, *Brown Girl, Brownstones* (New York, 1959)

Melville, Herman, 'Bartleby the Scrivener', in *The Piazza Tales* [1856] (New York, 1996)

Miller, Frank, *The Dark Knight* (New York, 1986)

O'Hara, Frank, *Collected Poems* (New York, 1971)

O'Neill, Joseph, *Netherland* (New York, 2008)

Ong, Han, *Fixer Chao* (New York, 2001)

Powell, Dawn, *The Locusts Have No King* (New York, 1948)

Price, Richard, *Lush Life* (New York, 2008)

Realuyo, Bino, *The Nuyorasian Anthology* (New York, 1999)

Roth, Henry, *Call It Sleep* (New York, 1991)

Salinger, J. D., *The Catcher in the Rye* (New York, 1945)

Selden, George, *The Cricket in Times Square* (New York, 1960)

Smith, Betty, *A Tree Grows in Brooklyn* (New York, 1947)

Stead, Rebecca, *When You Reach Me* (New York, 2009)

Taylor, Sydney, *All-of-a-Kind Family* (New York, 1978)

Wolfe, Tom, *The Bonfire of the Vanities* (New York, 1987)

Wharton, Edith, *The Age of Innocence* (New York, 1920)

White, E. B., *Stuart Little* (New York, 1945)

Whitman, Walt, *Complete Poetry and Collected Prose* (New York, 1982)

Non-fiction

Abbott, Berenice, and Bonnie Yochelson, *New York Changing: Revisiting Berenice Abbott's New York* (New York, 2005)

Bender, Thomas, *The Unfinished City: New York and the Metropolitan Idea* (Baltimore, MD, 1988)

Bradley, Elizabeth L., *Knickerbocker: The Myth behind New York* (New Brunswick, NJ, 2009)

Burns, Ric, and James Sanders, *New York: An Illustrated History* (New York, 1999)

Burroughs, Edwin, and Michael Wallace, *Gotham* (New York, 1999)

Dunbar, David, and Kenneth T. Jackson, eds, *Empire City: New York through the Centuries* (New York, 2002)

Fierstein, Sanna, *Naming New York: Manhattan Places and How they Got their Names* (New York, 2001)

Freeman, Joshua, *Working-class New York: Life and Labor since*

World War II (New York, 2001)

Jackson, Kenneth T., ed., *Encyclopedia of New York City* (New Haven, CT, 2010)

Koolhaas, Rem, *Delirious New York: A Retroactive Manifesto for Manhattan* (New York, 1994)

Kurlansky, Mark, *The Big Oyster* (New York, 2006)

Lopate, Phillip, *Writing New York: A Literary Anthology* (New York, 1998)

—, *Waterfront: A Journey Around Manhattan* (New York, 2004)

Mitchell, Joseph, *Up in the Old Hotel and Other Stories* (New York, 1992)

Morris, Jan, *Manhattan '45* (New York, 1987)

Patell, Cyrus, and Bryan Waterman, eds, *The Cambridge Companion to the Literature of New York* (New York, 2010)

Sanderson, Eric, *Mannahatta: A Natural History of New York City* (New York, 2009)

Santiago, Esmerelda, *When I was Puerto Rican* (New York, 1994)

Shorto, Russell, *The Island at the Center of the World: The Epic Story of Dutch Manhattan and the Forgotten Colony that Shaped America* (New York, 2004)

Spiegelman, Art, *In the Shadow of No Towers* (New York, 2004)

Sussman, Elisabeth, *City of Ambition: Artists and New York, 1900–1960* (New York, 1996)

Tippins, Sherill, *Inside the Dream Palace: The Life and Times of New York's Legendary Chelsea Hotel* (New York, 2013)

Walsh, Kevin, *Forgotten New York* (New York, 2006)

Wharton, Edith, *A Backward Glance* (New York, 1933)

White, E. B., *Here is New York* (New York, 1949)

Whitehead, Colson, *The Colossus of New York* (New York, 2003)

Websites

www.forgotten-ny.com
New York nostalgia, made fresh daily

www.gothamist.com
The unvarnished scoop on daily life in New York

www.hopstop.com
For public transit strategies and estimated travel times

www.nycgo.com
Official website of New York and Company, the city's tourist bureau

www.ny.eater.com
For food obsessives, includes tips on last-minute reservations at hot restaurants

www.timeout.com/newyork
Time Out New York's website, with all the city's event listings you could ever need

www.turnstiletours.com
Deeply researched and passionate tours of New York's ethnic enclaves, industrial history and cultural transformations, by bus, bicycle or on foot

Films

Man on Wire, dir. James Marsh (2008)
Manhatta, dir. Charles Sheeler and Paul Strand (1921)
New York: A Documentary Film, dir. Ric Burns (1999/2003)
On the Bowery, dir. Lionel Rogosin (1956)

Acknowledgements

I am grateful to my former colleagues at The New York Public Library, particularly Elaine Charnov, Paul Holdengraber, Lynda Kennedy, Jack Martin, Jean Strouse and Kelly Yim, for encouragement and inspiration at this project's inception, and to Kate Cordes and Matt Knutzen of the Library's Milstein Division of U.S. History, Local History and Genealogy for an opportunity to test my ideas in a public forum. David Ferriero, Archivist of the United States, and Ken Cobb, Director of the Municipal Archives of the City of New York, led me to amazing troves of New York images, and Michael Miscione, Jean-Gabriel Neukomm and Charlie O'Donnell shared their own extraordinary collections. Friends and family, including Aaron Beebe, John and Mary Lee Bradley, Joanna Ebenstein, Avery Fletcher, Mark Foggin, Philip Hollander, Troy Grady, Mandy Keifetz, Edward Knoblauch, Jessa Krick, Liz McEnaney, Karen Walton Morse, Judy Maxwell, Jacob Nadal, Adriana Nova, Sara Ogger, Juliet Page, Cyrus Patell, Andre Pennycooke, Andrew Shore, McKelden Smith and Cindy Vanden-Bosch enriched my Gotham knowledge immeasurably. The flaws in this book reflect only my own imperfect understanding and not their good counsel. Two wonderful families sustained me with seaside retreats: Samantha Karpel, Jared Katz and Indira Katz-Karpel; and Emily, Stevie, Siana and Bowen Solarazza. My agent, Wendy Strothman, and Reaktion's Cityscopes series editor, Vivian Constantinopoulos, embody the two qualities recommended by Fiorello LaGuardia to the citizens of New York – patience and fortitude. Mandy Keifetz (wearing her indexer's hat) made my small craft watertight. Finally, I wish to thank Eric Lai, who never lost sight of the wonders, weirdos and wheatpaste that brought him to New York in the first place and who, by his daily example, helps me to examine the present city with as much delighted interest (if not reverence) as I do the past.

Photo Acknowledgements

Courtesy of the 21 Club: p. 163; Alamy: p. 56 (Ivy Close Images); courtesy of the Bert Twaalfhoven Collection, Fordham University Library, Bronx, New York: p. 27; Elizabeth L. Bradley: pp. 36, 39, 42, 59, 62, 150, 153, 155, 158, 167, 174, 178, 192, 199, 211; Vivian Constantinopoulos: pp. 154, 208; Corbis: pp. 9 (Nathan Benn/ Ottochrome), 48, 117, 112 (Bettmann), 138–9 (Mario Pereda); Eli Duke: p. 160; courtesy of Friends of the High Line: p. 14; Getty Images: pp. 118 (De Agostini), 121 (Berenice Abbott); Mandy Goldberg: p. 198; courtesy of Historic Hudson Valley: p. 72; iStock-photo: p. 19 top (Lya_Cattel); Bob Jagendorf: p. 206; courtesy Jay Johnson, St Mark's Church in-the-Bowery: p. 34; Adam Jones, PhD: p. 171; courtesy Stacy Kovacs, Batala NYC: p. 187 (photo © Steven Sze); Eric Lai: pp. 190, 197, 207; Library of Congress, Washington, DC: p. 53, 55, 60, 61, 76, 77, 78, 79, 80–81, 84–5, 87, 88, 89, 93, 94, 96, 100, 101, 102, 108, 109, 122, 126, 127, 164; Marcus Melendez: p. 184; courtesy of the Metropolitan Museum of Art, New York: p. 202; collection of Michael Miscione: p. 98; courtesy of the Natural History Museum, New York: p. 203; © Jean-Gabriel Neukomm: p. 8; New York City Department of Transportation: p. 173; New York Municipal Archives: pp. 114, 142; New York Public Library: p. 40; Charlie O'Donnell: p. 194; Kristin Paulus: p. 166; Rex Features: pp. 11 bottom (Image Broker), 15 (WestEnd61), 18 top (MCT), 74 (Universal History Archive), 130, 137 (Everett Collection), 143 (Ted Polhemus/PYMCA); Paul Sableman: p. 183; Susan Semoneta: p. 169; Shutterstock: pp. 6–7 (Richard Cavalleri), 10 (Andrew F. Kazmierski), 11 top (Marcio Jose Bastos Silva), 12–13 (mandritoiu), 16 (Andreas Juergensemeier), 17 (Alan Kraft), 18 bottom (a katz), 19 bottom (Spirit of America), 20 (Martin Froyda), 29 (Kenneth Summers), 91 (EastVillage Images), 129 (Sean Pavone), 134 (littleny), 145 (Stuart

Monk), 176 (Evan Wong), 179 (Anthony Correia), 189 (Elzbieta Sekowska), 201 (Leonard Zukovsky), 204 (Manuel Hurtado); Calvin Snyder: p. 172; U.S. National Archives and Records Administration (NARA), Washington, DC: pp. 141 (Erik Calonius), 146; Will Vaultz Photography: p. 185; Alan Wu: pp. 180–81; Rebecca Zeller: p. 157.

Index

Page numbers in italics refer to illustrations